HOW TO BUY AND SELL GREAT BUSINESSES

WITHOUT RISKING YOUR OWN MONEY!

JONATHAN JAY

First published in Great Britain in 2017
Jonathan Jay and The Dealmakers Academy
c/o Causeway Law
6 Hays Lane
London Bridge
London
SE1 2HB

British Library Cataloguing in Publication Data.
ISBN 978-1-5272-1848-2

Contents

Introduction

Earlier this year, I signed a seven-figure deal for a company that I'd bought 11 months earlier for just £1. So, for a £1 investment, I received a seven-figure return. Any way you look at it, that's an incredible return on investment – the kind that share market investors can only dream about.

I want you to realise that you too can do the same. In this book, you'll discover how you can start buying and selling businesses for profit without risking your own money. By the time you finish, you'll realise that this is something you can do, and that it will have a hugely positive impact on your life and finances.

When I bought that company, with the intention of merging it with my own, it had an annual revenue of £4.7m. At the time, my own business was doing less than that in annual revenues; so, in one afternoon, I more than doubled my company's size.

You're probably wondering why, if it had an annual revenue of £4.7m, it sold for just £1. What was wrong with it?

It was a private equity-owned company and was 'unloved' – because it hadn't grown as quickly as its owners expected, they had all but lost interest in it. The company had a complicated ownership structure and had gone through several changes of management, which meant that the return on investment just wasn't there.

Even though it wasn't making any profit, I saw it as a worthwhile investment. To me, it represented what would have taken five or more years to achieve in that particular market.

Most importantly, I knew *why* it wasn't making any profit, and that I could fix it. So, I bought it and set about making it profitable. That mostly involved cost-cutting and removing overhead, so

- The management team's flashy company cars and big offices went.
- The expensive (but non-contributing) management team departed.
- The loss-making divisions were closed.
- Redundancies were made.
- Every penny was monitored.
- Some jobs were outsourced, and some were insourced.

Six months later, I had a £2m + EBITDA (earnings before interest, tax, depreciation and amortisation) company and decided to hire a broker to sell it. Nothing happened, so I sacked the broker and marketed it myself. I found a buyer and concluded a deal, just 11 months after buying the company.

I'm going to show you how to buy an underperforming, unloved company without using your own money, turn it around and sell it at an enormous profit. Or, you could keep it and build a portfolio of companies, if you want to.

How to create the wealth and get the freedom you want

The question you've probably been asking yourself for months, maybe years, is how can you escape from being an employee or consultant, working for a salary or a set fee? How can you get off the hamster wheel and start enjoying more wealth and more freedom?

If you own a business, growth might be slow or flat lining – this book is the answer to your problems.

You could buy a lottery ticket, but realistically, your chances of winning the jackpot are about one in 45 million (for the National Lottery) or one in 116.5 million (for the Euromillions Lottery).

You could set up a business using your own money or a bank loan and spend the next few years working 60–80-hour weeks, but still not get anywhere near the lifestyle and wealth you want. Worse, the chances of your startup surviving its first five years of operation are 50%. Although 80% of businesses survive their first year, 50% fail before their 5th anniversary. The sad truth is, only about 30% are still around to celebrate their 10th anniversary.

So, creating a startup is not an easy way to create the type of future you want.

What else could you do to improve your financial situation? You could invent a product that changes people's lives. But there again, even if you get funding for your invention, there's no guarantee you'll get any of the financial rewards. After all, many inventors like Sir Tim Berners-Lee, who invented the world wide web, and Rob Klein, who invented the magnetic credit card strip, made very little money from their creations.

So, if setting up a business, buying a lottery ticket, inventing a product or just running your existing business aren't the solutions, what is? What *can* you do that will help you attain your goals of freedom and unlimited wealth?

The answer is you can become what I call a 'dealmaker' – someone who buys and sells businesses to make a profit without ever risking his or her own money. You're going to discover how to be a dealmaker. Right now, this may seem impossible, but I'm about to provide you with a blueprint that you can follow. It's a step-by-step process that I use and which will help you achieve your dream of financial freedom, regardless of your current situation.

Right now there's probably a little voice in your mind that's saying:

'I don't have the funds to buy a business.'
'I don't have any experience in running a business.'
'I don't know much about other markets or industries.'

Here's what I have learnt from my experience of being a dealmaker – you don't need previous experience or a gazillion pounds in the bank to become a dealmaker. You don't need an encyclopaedic knowledge of every market and industry. You can research and find out enough to do deals. You don't need a degree in business administration or accounting to become a dealmaker. You can hire experts to take care of the numbers as well as the all-important tax details and legalities for you. You can hire a management team to take care of the day-to-day operations for you.

What's important is that you can buy the businesses without using and, therefore, without risking any of your own money. Better yet, you'll be able to withdraw a monthly fee and annual dividend as well as enjoy a big payday when you sell your businesses.

This will give you the freedom and lifestyle that very few people get to enjoy.

The advantages of being a dealmaker

Why would anyone want to be a dealmaker rather than a business owner, an employee or the founder of a startup business?

As a dealmaker, you avoid the stress of setting up a business and taking it through its early development. Someone has already done that for you.

You don't take the financial risk that the original owner took to set up a new business. Quite often, startup owners use their own money or borrow funds from family members and friends to finance the startup.

Why aren't there more dealmakers?

I think there are two reasons why more people aren't doing deals like this. First, they regard it as cheating because it's not the endless years of hard work that most business owners endure. It's not cheating. It's a way to get what you want faster. Second, they don't know how to do it. They think it's very complex.

Delegates at my seminars often say, *'I didn't realise buying and selling businesses was so straightforward, but now that it's been explained to me, I get it'.*

It's like watching David Copperfield or David Blain perform magic on TV. You sit there and wonder how on earth they did the trick. A little while later, you see a video on YouTube that explains how they did it. Suddenly, you realise it's very straightforward. You think to yourself, 'I could do that.'

By the time you've finished reading this book, you'll have the same realisation. Buying and selling businesses *is* straightforward; it is something you can start doing immediately (I'm so certain you can that as well as the 12-step process I've included a 50-point Action Plan to encourage you to take action as soon as you've finished reading the book).

Why should you believe what I'm telling you?

The simple answer is I've done it, and I continue to do so. Over the years, I've bought and sold about 25 differently sized businesses. A few of them sold for a few hundred thousand and others for millions of pounds.

My focus now is on creating multi-million-pound exits. That's not to decry exits that are worth less than that. After all, a day in which £150k arrives in your bank account is a day worthy of celebration!

The reason why I'm focused on multi-million-pound exits is that I've discovered that the same amount of effort goes into selling a large business as a small business. Actually, selling a small business can sometimes be tougher than selling a larger one.

I've also discovered that buying and selling other people's businesses is just as exciting as starting and growing my own businesses. It's also much easier and far more profitable. You will make more money buying and selling businesses than you ever will from running one.

Think about it: there are very few ways of getting the kind of huge return I received on my £1 investment in just 11 months. Of course, I must add a disclaimer here: not every business will generate this kind of ROI. And not every business can be bought and sold in under 12 months (but I'm going to show you how to pick companies that will be easier to sell than others).

Being a dealmaker has brought me the rewards and freedom I want without the stresses that running start-up companies involved.

If you compare business owners with dealmakers, business owners take all the financial risk. They borrow the money, they secure it against their homes, they take the personal guarantees. They also do all the hard work; they're the first person to arrive in the morning and the last person to leave at night. They're the ones who pop into the office on the weekends and find it impossible to stop thinking about the business.

But dealmakers don't have the financial risk, and they don't have the worry. They don't sign personal guarantees or put their homes on the line. They do comparatively little work than startup business owners.

So, when you become a dealmaker the potential for failure is low. That's because you buy a business that has worked, maybe not as well as it could have, but it has worked for at least five years. The second thing is, you're not going to buy just one business, you're going to have half a dozen of them. Just like you don't buy one Buy to Let, but half a dozen of them to spread the risk.

Let's say, heaven forbid, something does happen to one of those businesses, it won't matter because you will have other businesses that will take the strain. Your goal is to take a monthly £10,000 consulting fee out of every business you own. If you own two businesses, then that's £20,000 a month. Three businesses? That's £30,000 a month, and so on. Now you're probably seeing why owning several businesses is advantageous!

I spent the first few weeks after buying the £1 business working on it full time. The business needed some TLC in those early days. However, before long, I was able to reduce my hours. Then, of course, I received a nice big cheque when I sold it 11 months later. That made it a very nice year.

Now, I own a luxury villa in Marbella with the money I made on that deal. Not bad for something that began with a £1 investment!

Until I became a dealmaker, I had been an entrepreneur. From the age of 12, I'd set up and run businesses. I created and ran two other businesses that I subsequently sold for seven figures (The Coaching Academy and The Marketing Guild).

For many years, I loved being an entrepreneur so much that I encouraged other people to leave their day jobs and become entrepreneurs too. I spoke at hundreds of seminars and even wrote a book in 2004 called *Sack Your Boss!* about how to start a business.

But after discovering the many benefits of being a dealmaker, I resolved to never start a new company again. Why the change of heart? Well, because I found that being a dealmaker provides me with more financial and personal success than being an entrepreneur, and it's a great deal less stressful!

If you have never created a business, you might not realise how stressful and risky running a startup can be. Yes, it's exciting, but it's also enormously challenging. You face cash flow issues, hassles with getting the product or service to match your customers' expectations and problems with managing people. Your savings are drained, and you spend every available hour working or thinking about your business.

It's likely that you end up getting less money than you would in a salaried position and yet, you spend more time at the office than at home. And there's the very real prospect that the business you've spent money, time and energy nurturing from inception won't last more than five years.

All in all, it's the opposite of what you hoped would happen when you first set up the business.

It was after I'd sold my third company that I realised that I'd gone through the same three phases with my companies.

- **Phase One:** The years when it's all work and no money.
- **Phase Two:** The years when it's all work and some money – unpredictable and irregular.
- **Phase Three:** The exit, when there's a burst of activity for 16 weeks, then more money than I had ever earned during Phase Two (which might have lasted for five years more).

I had burnt myself out, but hardly earned anything for years, then worked incredibly hard for an irregular income for the next few years and finally hit the jackpot when I sold the business to someone else.

That's why a few years ago I decided to do things differently. Instead of starting another business, I bought one in which someone else had taken it through Phase One. Someone else had invested the capital, proven the concept, done the marketing, built the client base and worked seven days a week for years.

Nowadays, when a business enters Phase Two, and the irregular and unpredictable income has taken its toll on the business owner, I enter the picture as the dealmaker. I help the business owner by bringing fresh energy and new ideas to their company. I either buy the business or at least a large share of it as an investor, not an owner-manager.

The beauty of investing in someone else's company means you can leapfrog both the start-up phase and the hard-work phase.

You can buy a company in which someone else has proven the business model. You do this without risking any of your own money (or your home) or taking out expensive bank loans. You don't get bogged down in the day-to-day running of the company.

And you can share in the upside and help the owner engineer a profitable exit for the both of you.

In other words, you can still have all the emotional pleasures of owning a business without the stress and anguish of the *'Will it/Won't it work?'* phase.

The role of the dealmaker is to add value by coming in with a fresh set of eyes and spotting the missed opportunities and the wasted money as well as keeping the management focused on the bigger picture.

Usually, business owners sell you equity with pleasure, delight and relief because they are struggling, and they know you can take their business to Phase Three – the exit.

You can still help it grow and have the satisfaction of its success, but without having to deal with staff issues, administration or customer service.

In other words, you can be a business owner of a 'ready-made' business without the financial risk, but with all the upsides.

If that sounds appealing, read on to discover how to do it.

Creating Your Perfect Life

Before we delve into how you are going to make deals, you need to decide why you want to do it and what you hope to achieve. What kind of lifestyle do you want? What is your idea of a perfect life?

Let's start by looking at your current financial situation. Are you happy with where you are right now? Or do you feel you should be better off?

Consider for a moment how many years you've been working. Now rate your current financial situation on a scale of one to ten (with ten being 'I'm wealthy beyond my dreams'). How much effort have you taken in your working life on a scale of one to ten (with ten being you've been at it like a crazy person for 25 years, or whatever it might be).

When I ask business owners at my seminars to do this exercise, they're often amazed at how low their satisfaction with their financial situation is and how much effort they've put into their business. They typically rate their financial success below a five and their effort at nine or ten. Not many people say, *'I didn't put any effort into my business'*.

If you're working at a nine or a ten in terms of effort, you can't go any higher. You simply can't. Working longer hours is not going to create bigger financial results. If the hours you worked equalled the money that you had in the bank, then most people would be multi-millionaires simply because they'd put in so much effort. But that's not how it is. So just working harder isn't the answer. I believe dealmaking is the answer.

Before you become a dealmaker, you need to have a strategy, and that will be determined by what you want your life to be like. Your vision of your ideal life will be unique to you. What does the outcome that you want look like? What would make your life perfect (or way better than it is now)? How will you improve your finances with less effort and more fun?

Consider the following aspects of your life.

Working life

What would your perfect working life be like in terms of

- Working hours;
- Commute;
- Location;
- Workspace; and
- Managing or delegating jobs.

Personal life

What would your perfect personal life be like regarding

- Family time;
- Leisure time;
- Travel;
- Home;
- Passions; and
- Your big dream.

Financial life

What would your perfect financial situation be like regarding

- Disposable income;
- Savings;

- Commitments; and
- Funding projects or charities.

How will you get from where you are now to where you want to be?

What will you need to achieve in the next 12 months? The next three years? Five years? Ten years? The year you decide to retire?

What is your projected income this year, and how many hours will you have to work to achieve it? Divide the number of hours you will have to work into your projected income to discover your hourly rate.

Now, think of the income level you'd like to achieve next year. How many hours will you work to achieve that income? Divide the number of hours into your projected income to calculate your hourly rate.

What is the difference between the two hourly rates?

The Mindset and Attitude of a Dealmaker

To succeed as a dealmaker, you must want more than a job. When you buy a business the way I'm going to show you, it's not about securing a job for life. It's about buying a vehicle that you can use to improve your current finances and lifestyle. The business will be there to serve you and provide you with the lifestyle and financial rewards you want. You will not be there to serve the business. Understanding this is crucial to your success as a dealmaker.

It's up to you to decide whether to

- Run the business;
- Retain an existing management team;
- Parachute in a management team – maybe someone you meet at one of my seminars;
- Consolidate the new business with your existing business; or
- Strip and sell off the assets of the new business – a quick 'flip'.

What does it take to be a successful dealmaker?

The traits of the dealmaker are probably very different from what you expect. You might think that you must be brash and aggressive like Gordon Gecko from *Wall Street* or Jordan Belfort from *The Wolf of Wall Street*. That's far from reality.

One of the most effective traits of a dealmaker is the ability to get along with people. If you want people to sell you their business, you've got to be a nice person, so they want to do the deal with you.

Most successful dealmakers are

- Honest. Being a successful dealmaker isn't about screwing people over on deals. It's about buying or selling a business, so both sides get what they want (or as near to it as possible).

- Hard working and focused. You will need to work in a very focused way on your business. In the beginning, you might put in a 35-hour week as you ensure that costs are cut and improvements are made. The amount you work on the business will decrease as things improve.

  You will also need to spend time finding more deals.

- Respectful. A great dealmaker won't patronise or insult other buyers or sellers, but make it clear they respect them. You might think, 'Oh come on, if the deal's right, they'll snap it up regardless of what I'm like.'

  That's not the case. There's so much emotion when people sell a business. They want to sell it to people they like. You've got to tell them what a great job they've done. Okay, they've hit a bit of a hard time because of the recession, but that isn't their fault. Tell them how you can take the business to the next level. You'll be amazed with how pleased people are that you're not intending to asset strip their business and close it down.

- Good with people. If you're abrasive or patronising, prospective sellers won't want to deal with you. They want to know that you're going to look after the businesses they have created from scratch.

- Decisive. Dealmakers don't spend months deliberating over a deal. For example, I have someone who can carry out due diligence on any company I'm considering and report back to me within 24 hours on whether it's worth proceeding. They'll call me and say, 'Jonathan, this is something you should be doing', or 'Jonathan, walk away, you're wasting your time on this one.' It saves me a lot of time. I'm a decisive person, but when there are multiple deals in the pipeline, it helps to have someone else running the numbers for me.

- Quick to act. When people decide to sell a business, they want to move fast, so you need to act quickly, which means you need to have the right team around you and have the right documentation prepared. You need to be able to move quickly through the purchase process because if you drag the process out, the deal can fall over. There's something called 'deal fatigue'. When negotiations drag on endlessly, both parties begin to get exhausted, frustrated and irritated by the process. They begin to lose hope that they will ever reach an agreement. There's a risk that the deal will collapse, or the seller will decide to consider other alternatives such as putting a manager in place rather than selling it.
- Responsible. If you're buying businesses that have staff, and you will be because there's no point buying a business without staff unless you're buying its intellectual property assets (IP), you need to have a sense of responsibility. People's livelihoods are at stake. You have to respect that those people have families and financial obligations like mortgages or rents to pay and endeavour to treat them fairly. However, you may need to cut overheads by making some of those employees redundant, and it's much better to do that quickly and respectfully.

The right way of doing this is to use the services of a great HR person who understands what you're trying to do. You need someone to whom you can say, 'I need to reduce the headcount; we need to get rid of "x" number of people, and we need to do it quickly and painlessly. Could you do all the paperwork and make sure there's no comeback on me. I don't want any issues. I want this done professionally, and I don't want anyone to feel they've been short-changed.'

I made 70 people redundant from a company I bought last year. With the help of my HR person, we did it almost without any issues. The one issue we had was with someone who'd been to a job interview and been offered the job. Bizarrely, he'd been sent an employment contract to sign before he started working there. Personally, I wouldn't offer anyone an employment contract before they'd been with my company for some weeks. I'd want to see how they performed before offering them a contract. But in this case, we had to pay this man for a job he hadn't even started.

- Capable of letting go and delegating. This will get easier as you buy more companies because you'll come to realise that you have to keep your eye on the big picture and allow other people to take care of the day-to-day running of the business.

Dealmaking myths

There are plenty of myths surrounding dealmakers. But they're just that – myths.

Let me debunk a few of them right now.

Myth*: You need a large cash reserve to buy other businesses.*

Reality: You don't need a large cash reserve because you won't be using your own money to finance the deal.

Myth*: You need a perfect credit history.*

Reality: You don't need to have a perfect credit history because you won't be approaching banks or lending institutions to buy businesses.

Myth*: Only big businesses or big players can buy out other businesses.*

Reality: Individuals can buy businesses just as easily as multinational conglomerates can. Sometimes it's easier for individuals because owners know that you can do the deal quickly and it won't take months of internal meetings for you to be in a position to buy.

Likewise, you don't need to operate out of an office to be a dealmaker. You can sit in your lounge with a laptop and do it all from there. I'm buying shares in a business near London Bridge that has a lovely office with a meeting room. So, I'm going to hold meetings there. If I need to go and sit somewhere, then I'll go and sit in their office. So you don't need an office, you can use the offices of the businesses that you're acquiring, or in this case, investing in.

Myth: *You'll work yourself to the bone.*

Reality: Being a dealmaker means you can structure your lifestyle to suit your needs and wants. When you're the sole trader of a start-up, this is almost never the case. You have to be available 24/7. That's why I strongly recommend that you don't get into the habit of turning up every day or even week at the offices of the companies you buy. Let your manager or management team run it for you. Yes, you should attend a monthly board meeting, but you can hold that meeting anywhere: in your front room or a hotel foyer down the road. In other words, you don't have to get sucked into the daily running of any business you buy.

If you are in the office every day, something is wrong. You're not allowing your manager or management team to do their job and are probably getting in the way.

Myth: *It's very complicated, and you need to be a financial whizz to know what you're doing.*

Reality: You don't have to be a financial genius to be a successful dealmaker. First, I'm going to show you how to do deals. Second, you can hire experts to help you get the best possible deal. I have a team of people whom I pay to help me analyse, buy, grow and sell businesses. My team includes experts in finance, tax, law and HR. Unless you have expertise in each of these areas, I strongly recommend you do the same – hire a team. Don't try to wing it!

Myth: *Negotiating deals is hard.*

Reality: As a dealmaker, you'll be negotiating with business owners. No matter what you might think, negotiating is not difficult. Every day I receive emails from business owners who want to meet to discuss the purchase of their businesses. How much negotiating does that require? None. People offer me their businesses.

Why it isn't all about the money

Being a dealmaker is more than just earning a very good income. It's about freedom: the freedom to decide how you spend your time and energy. The freedom to live where you want. The freedom to control your income. And the freedom to control your future.

Of course, that doesn't mean you won't be working hard occasionally. You will. You'll just be doing it to achieve your most desired outcome rather than someone else's.

Possible outcomes

Depending on your goals, you can achieve many things as a dealmaker. Things that you can never do if you are an employee.

For example, you could make one deal that completely changes your life and allows you to retire early.

Or you could own a portfolio of businesses that generate a steady income stream for however long you want to hold onto them.

You could get involved as much or as little as you want in the running of the businesses.

Obviously, there are going to be elements of becoming a dealmaker that appeal to you. They might be

- You'll work less;
- You'll have more money;
- You'll be able to 'switch off' instead of carrying the stresses of running a business around with you;
- You'll have less risk (because if you have more than one business, you won't be dependent on one business, one job or one client for your income); and
- You'll be able to dramatically grow your business' size if you 'bolt on' another business to it.

There are probably elements of being a dealmaker that still worry you. You might think

- You'll have trouble sourcing businesses to buy.
- You'll make mistakes.

Let me put your mind at rest right now: buyers really do call the shots in this market. At any given time, there are half a million businesses for sale. There are always more sellers than buyers. What's more, it's going to continue to be the case for years to come since 63% of small business owners are over the age of 50. At some point, those owners will be looking to exit their businesses.

About two-thirds of those business owners don't have a succession plan. Some are so consumed with trying to grow their business that they don't have time to formulate an effective exit plan. Others think they are so indispensable that no one else could do the same job. And some haven't found suitable candidates to replace them. For those who do have a plan, they envisage selling the business to a third party or a chosen key employee or family member.

So you aren't going to have a problem sourcing businesses to buy.

Case Study One: The Coaching Academy

In 1999, I set up what would become the UK's first life coaching school. I'd attended a seminar of 500 people in which an American life coach addressed the audience. At the time, I was publishing a personal development magazine, so I was there to get more subscribers. The magazine was losing money, so I was desperate to find more subscribers.

While I was there, I discovered that about 400 of the people in the audience were interested in training to be life coaches.

Sensing this was a fantastic opportunity, I rushed back to my office and wrote the advertising copy for a two-day coach training event.

I contacted a colleague who owned a personal development mailing list with 12,000 names on it and asked him to carry a postcard insert that would advertise the training event. I spent £145 I hadn't got, having 10,000 direct response postcards printed targeting people on his subscriber list who might be interested in life coaching.

I couldn't afford to fund a Freepost address at the time since I had a business overdraft that was nudging £20,000 and was receiving daily phone calls from my bank manager who reminded me I was nearing my overdraft limit. So, anyone who was interested in receiving more information had to buy a stamp and send their response to a rented mailing address in Bedford Square, London. The mail was forwarded to my office in Portsmouth.

Within days of the publication landing on people's doorsteps, we were swamped with hundreds and hundreds of enquiries. I'd included a Freephone number, and the calls went through to a centre where staff took messages and then faxed them through to the office.

Business just rolled in. Within a matter of days, 27 people had each paid £2,000 to attend the training event.

My bank manager, who'd been away on holiday while all this was going on, rang me on his first day back in the office. 'Jonathan,' he said, 'I think there's something wrong with your account – it's gone from being nearly £20,000 in the red to £20,000 in the black.' That was a terrific moment!

I then set about creating the training course. I found five experts on life coaching, and we put together a two-day training course so the people who'd paid for the course could become life coaches.

On Saturday, October 16, 1999, at a country hotel near Coventry in the West Midlands, those 27 people arrived to attend the coach training session.

It wasn't actually until Monday morning when the phone kept ringing with people asking when the next course was, that I realised I had the opportunity to do it repeatedly. I had no idea that there was scope to do more than one training course, but the timing was perfect: there was an unsatisfied demand for coach training that many people had recognised, but never done anything about.

I even found a buyer for the personal development magazine I'd been publishing, which was still losing money.

He ran it for three issues and then folded it because it didn't make any money for him either.

But by then, The Coaching Academy was doing so well that I gave the payment cheque for the magazine to my parents as a gift.

Within the first 12 months, the Academy had turned over £1m and continued to grow.

At a course in 2001, a delegate said he'd like to buy the company for £1m.

I was so surprised. I hadn't considered that anyone would want to buy it because to me, it was a beast of a business and I was having to learn things that I didn't have much experience with, like managing staff and finances.

I turned him down. Later I discovered one of the trainers had approached the prospective buyer and suggested they set up their own coaching training company, which they did. It became the

UK College of Life Coaching, and within the space of a week, half my training team and half my sales team had jumped ship.

Worse, my former trainer began emailing our customers.

I responded by launching a marketing tsunami. When you are proactively marketing, you're reaching thousands and thousands of people who would never have encountered one of your existing customers, so marketing helps it grow far faster than if you allowed it to grow organically.

Over the next few years, the same prospective buyer came back to me a few times and asked me to sell. I kept turning him down. Eventually, he asked, 'What do you want for it?' I replied, 'I want £5 million.' My lawyer was with me and afterwards said to me, 'I think the guy's all talk. I don't think it's going to go through.'

But I was very naïve and thought the prospective buyer was serious. I handed over all the information he requested. He asked lots of questions about the business and of course, I was cooperative because I believed he was genuinely interested. The whole thing just fizzled out.

I realised later that it was just a fishing expedition. It was just a way of him finding out what we were doing differently and more successfully than his company.

A few years later, I received a phone call from that same prospective buyer inviting me to a meeting at a hotel near his office in Wolverhampton. 'Here we go again', I thought.

During the meeting, he offered to sell me his business. I was delighted because his company had become a real thorn in our side. We agreed to a deal there and then. It was a Monday afternoon, and we signed the contract that Friday, so within five days I owned his company's assets – for pennies.

It was all done very, very rapidly. What I didn't know was that the company was in so much financial difficulty it was about to be passed to administrators. Fortunately, I didn't buy the liabilities: they stayed with the company and were then wound up by the administrators.

I have to admit that emotion massively motivated my purchase. I was afraid that if I didn't make a move, someone else would snap up the deal.

The logical thing would have been to research the situation, and then I would have discovered it was about to go into administration. I could then have allowed it to go into administration and picked it up for even less than what I paid.

Fortunately, I'd listened to my lawyer who advised me to buy only the assets, not the shares. If I'd bought the shares, I would have been left with £1m in liabilities.

The following Monday morning, I went to the office in Wolverhampton and interviewed the staff. Some people resigned on the spot; such was the enmity between our two companies. I retained two members of staff and made the rest redundant.

The bailiffs arrived that morning ready to seize the company's assets, but I told them the assets were mine since I'd bought them. I then closed the Wolverhampton office and moved everything down to London.

We diverted all the phone lines to our London office and diverted the web traffic to our website. So effectively, if someone phoned them or emailed them they got us.

Interestingly, I found that a copy of my database was on the office server. No attempt had been made to disguise the fact that it was taken from us because it was labelled, 'Coaching Academy Database'.

Purchasing the UK College of Life Coaching showed me that you could grow your business by acquiring a competitor. It had been making about £1m in sales while we were making between £3m and £4m. As soon as we removed them from the marketplace, our sales went up by £1m because we scooped up their sales. I had the Coaching Academy business valued before the acquisition, and it was worth about £2.5m, and about a year afterwards, it was valued at £5m – simply because I had bought my bust competitor.

Selling the Coaching Academy

I decided to sell the company on January 1st, 2007. I was standing outside a shop in Monte Carlo, waiting for my girlfriend and enviously looking at people relaxing at outdoor café tables, sipping wine in the sunshine. I thought 'I want more of that. I'm getting stressed by this business.' I decided at that moment to sell the business.

It took nearly 11 months to accomplish. I signed the sales contract on November 17th, 2007.

A few months previously, I'd signed an agreement with a business broker, but I hadn't done anything because I was so busy doing other things. So I went back to him and said, 'Okay, let's put the business on the market.'

His company advertised it along with lots of other companies in different newspapers. I didn't know it at the time, but this was actually how the bottom end of the business sales market works. Our multi-million-pound business was advertised alongside fish-and-chip shops and corner shops. It was completely inappropriate. It was also undervalued.

The broker behaved more like an introduction agency than a professional business broker because whenever prospective buyers contacted him, he just directed them to me. It was crazy. I was meeting prospective buyers in hotel lobbies all over the country. The Information Memorandum, the document containing all the information about the business, was very poorly constructed.

I realised after a while that a sale wasn't going to happen. The people I'd met were time wasters.

In the meantime, I had withdrawn my involvement in the business to demonstrate that it worked fine without me at the helm. I removed myself from all the promotional material and stopped going to training events and meeting customers. I delegated everything to make myself redundant.

After failing to find a buyer, I began to rethink my decision to sell. I thought if I wasn't going to sell, maybe I should buy. I found a publication that advertised businesses for sale, and there was a section on training businesses. So I phoned up one of the training businesses because I thought the Coaching Academy could become an NVQ provider.

The guy who answered asked me to tell him about my business. I did, and he said, 'Those numbers are amazing.'

I told him I was more interested in selling the business, but at the same time, I was thinking about buying other businesses to bolt onto it.

He said, 'Well if you want to sell it, I'll represent you because I just focus on training businesses. I used to run a training business, that's what I know. I specialise in training businesses.'

I waited until the contract with the business broker had expired and then went back to the new broker and asked him to manage the sale.

We had far more successful meetings than I'd had with the previous company. He came with me and did most of the talking.

The turning point came when he arranged a meeting at a small private equity firm. We met on a Monday afternoon. There were two people from the private equity company plus an individual who wanted to run the Coaching Academy on their behalf.

By Friday afternoon, we had agreed on Heads of Terms. They were broadly acceptable, and about 120 days later, the company was sold. The deal was worth £7m of which I got £5m on completion with a further £2m if certain targets were hit.

In hindsight, I think the business was badly positioned. I should have hired a corporate finance company to front the sale rather than an individual. I didn't appreciate what a strong business it was, and because I didn't appreciate that no-one else did.

There are several takeaways from this experience. First, don't buy or sell when you're emotionally involved. It's a huge mistake. Second, look for competitors that you can snap up. Third, don't be fooled into thinking that because a company has flashy offices and a website they're doing well. Examine the financials. That's what's important.

Case Study: The Marketing Guild

Something that had become more apparent to me was how small to medium-sized companies really struggled with attracting and converting leads. Many had terrible marketing and as a result, had trouble getting consistent sales.

So, a few months after I'd sold The Coaching Academy, I started a marketing training company, which offered business owners seminars and mastermind groups. We taught them how to use the internet to attract, convert and retain clients. Then, instead of offering training, we were offering a 'done-for-you' service where we offered a contract to take care of all the digital marketing for companies for a year or more.

It was a great business. I ran it for seven or eight years, but always with the intention of selling it. I received two offers, one that was £21m, and one that was £15.5m. Now by this stage, I'd sold 50% of the company's shares to someone who had a huge database, which I knew we could use to get more clients.

Unfortunately, the shareholders' agreement that we both signed was very poor. I made a mistake, and it ended up costing me millions of pounds. Instead of going to my usual lawyer to draw up the shareholders' agreement, I decided to save money and get it done cheaply. Someone said, 'Oh, go to this chap, he'll do it for you for next to nothing.' It cost between £1k to £2k. If I'd gone to my usual lawyer, it might have cost me between £8k to £10k. That might seem like a lot, but not when millions of pounds are at stake.

By the time we put the business on the market, my relationship with my partner had fractured to the point where we were barely talking. Unfortunately, our shareholders' agreement did not have a deadlock provision. Such a provision or procedure is usually set out to resolve situations like ours in which shareholders have an irreconcilable conflict, but neither shareholder has a majority (because each has 50% of the company's shares) and serious disagreements have arisen over managing the business. The provisions might have included a Russian roulette clause, an auction clause, arbitration, or an agreement to liquidate the company.

Without such a provision, we had to continue. We received two offers for the company. The £21m offer was from a very well-known and active private equity firm. It was a deal that looked incredible. But there was a challenge. They said, 'It's £10.5m cash and £10.5m in shares. Those shares then crystallise in value upon a secondary buyout at some point in the future.'

The catch was that my estranged colleague would receive the cash, and I'd get the shares but no cash. I declined the deal. I wanted cash too. For that reason, the offer of £15.5m from another private equity firm seemed better.

When it got to Heads of Terms, my partner wouldn't agree to the anti-compete clause. Now, when you sell a business, you normally have to agree that you're not going to compete with the business that you've just sold.

He wouldn't sign the non-compete agreement even though he said he wasn't going to compete. I said, 'Well, sign the non-compete.' He refused.

So the deal fell apart. Finally, after many more months, I offered to buy back his shares.

He asked for £10.5m.

I said, 'No.'

So he came back and asked for £5m. His offer kept going down until it was just a few thousand pounds. Finally, I bought back the shares for next to nothing.

Case Study Three: SEO Company

During the negotiations, I decided I needed a Plan B. I thought, 'I can't sit around here doing nothing.' I remembered that one of the business owners we'd approached to buy the business had responded by saying he was looking for a buyer for his business.

I went onto LinkedIn, which is a great resource for dealmaking, and realised I was connected with the company's marketing director. We arranged to meet. Over coffee, I said, 'I wonder what our business would look like if we combined your balance sheet with our balance sheet. Wouldn't that be quite an impressive business?'

Our products were selling for £10k, £20k and £30k, while theirs were selling at much lower prices. He said, 'Well, it sounds very good, but you're talking to the wrong person. You need to speak to the CEO.'

I asked him to introduce us. A few weeks later, the CEO came to our office for a chat.

He said, 'We're owned by a private equity firm, and we're coming up to the end of the fund life. And they want to do something with the business. Are you interested in buying it?'

'I might be…if the deal is right', I said.

'But I've got to tell you', he said, 'if you look at our balance sheet and the management accounts, it's not going to look great because there's a lot of loan notes in there. There are fees back to the private equity firm that haven't been paid. It's not going to look great.'

I said, 'Okay, fine, I understand that.'

It was making £4.7m in revenue, but not making any profit. I knew that there were too many employees and the costs were out of control. The salaries for the executive team was about £650k a year. The executive team all drove Porsches and other similar cars. They all had assistants, and those assistants had assistants. I worked all this out, and it came to about £800k. I thought, 'Well if they all go, I'd make £800,000 profit in day one.'

Why didn't those guys in the executive team do that?

The only way to save the company and make it profitable was for them to all quit, which they weren't going to do. They were on £110k or £120k a year each. They were the wrong people to sort the business out.

When I analysed what the company was offering, I saw that there were loss-making elements. For example, they offered web design. I know web design is a tough and highly competitive market. This company had a loss-making web design element, but justified it because it was the front end of its search engine optimisation (SEO) offering.

Its social media and video services were also loss-makers. Then I saw there was £3m recurring revenue paid by direct debits. That part of the business was SEO, and pay-per-click (PPC) advertising, which can be hugely profitable. I'd never been involved with SEO, but I knew it to be hugely profitable.

The business also owed HMRC £1m from Employee Benefit Trusts and film partnerships.

Armed with this information, I went to a meeting and said, 'I realise that you've got some HMRC problems and if I'm going to take on all these responsibilities, I can't pay you for taking on your debts.'

They said, 'Well, you've got to convince all the shareholders to accept the same deal because a deal that you offer to one shareholder has to be offered to everyone else.' There were 37 shareholders. I went up and down the country to meet all 37 of the shareholders.

I explained that their shares in the company were virtually worthless because it was about to go into administration, but I was willing to buy them for £1.

They also had millions of pounds of loan notes owed to the shareholders that I bought for £1 too.

I restructured the debt. I had all the assets valued by a third-party valuer and paid that amount. That value was distributed to the creditors.

It took 12 weeks to put together the deal with this company, and it was a little complicated because we were buying it from a private equity firm. It doesn't have to take that long. Sometimes you can do an asset deal in days.

To do deals like this, you must use the services of highly experienced accountants and lawyers. You shouldn't attempt to do this by yourself. You can't rip a template off the internet and hope to achieve a great deal. You do need to have legal advice and ensure that you're doing everything properly.

Some lawyers will demand their fees upfront, whereas others may be happy to invoice after the deal is completed. If that happens, you can pay your legal fees using money from the business. You may be able to make a contingent deal in which you only pay legal fees if the deal completes. If the deal falls apart, you don't pay the entire bill. A 100% contingent deal is rare, but there's usually an abort fee.

Back to the loss-making business. After we'd restructured the business, it was making £2m + EBITDA per annum. We didn't add a single customer to achieve that. We actually lost customers. We also got rid of four franchise operations because they cost the business £40k a month. Some of the franchisees took a few customers with them, but it didn't matter. We still had a £2m profit business with £3m recurring revenue.

How long would it take for someone to take a startup through to a £2m profit? Forever! Very few businesses in the UK make a £1m profit. I had a £2m business, and it was all because of spotting an opportunity and acting on it.

I also had a professional team, with whom I could talk through ideas and issues. It helps, when it comes to making decisions, to have people with whom you can consult and discuss things.

Eleven months after buying that business, I sold it for an excellent seven-figure sum.

Now, I'm going to show you how you too can make fantastic deals like that. By following the 12-step blueprint in the next section, you'll find dealmaking straightforward and entirely within your reach. My aim is to give you the confidence and knowledge to complete your first deal.

The 12-Step Blueprint for Buying and Selling Businesses

How to find, fund, fix and flip within a dozen moves

STEP 1
Clarify your Dealmaking Strategy

You will have skills that you can use to raise the value of the business you buy. They might be hard skills such as the following:

- Sales (You know how to attract and retain customers);
- Marketing (You understand how to create marketing systems, unearth hidden profits, and increase the lifetime value of clients);
- Finance (You can negotiate with creditors and debtors);
- Operations and Logistics (You can streamline processes);
- IT (You can systematise operations, automate processes, and introduce reporting); and
- HR (You can manage layoffs, and attract and retain top performers).

Or they might be soft skills such as the following:

- People management;
- Motivating staff;
- Building rapport with staff, customers and suppliers;
- Team building; and
- Effecting cultural change, communicating your vision for the business and winning hearts and minds.

Which hard or soft skills do you have that you can use to boost the value of any business you buy? You might look at a business and say, 'You know what, they've got the wrong people in the wrong jobs. Half these people are just useless at what they're doing; they're just not right for this company and really shouldn't be here. Let's find the right people.' Then you hire the right people and put them in the right jobs; the business just takes off as a result.

Maybe you're brilliant at inspiring employees to unite for a common goal. Perhaps you're fantastic at accountancy, or you're brilliant at marketing.

If you have great rapport-building skills, you could visit some of the company's former clients. You could say, 'I'm the new owner. Maybe if you give us a second chance, we can prove to you that we're the right company to help you solve your biggest problem.'

The thing is, with some businesses, a single customer might be worth hundreds of thousands of pounds; so, if you win just one back, it might be enough to turn the business around.

If you're great at effecting cultural change, you could lift employee morale. It could be at rock bottom because employees will have picked up on the fact that the business is failing. So when you take over the business, you could say, 'We know we've got lots of competitors out there. We know that we used to be right there at the top, and that we've slipped down the ladder. Our goal in the next 12 months is to take us back to the number one position, but we can't do it without your help.'

Obviously, it takes more than a speech to lift employee morale, but you want to show from the outset that you have a vision for the business and they are part of that. It's about winning hearts and minds.

There will be aspects of being a dealmaker that you hate or in which you don't have any expertise. I'm not great at hiring people, for example. I hire people that I like in the interview and afterwards, realise that they can't do the job. To remedy that, I let other people do the hiring on my behalf because I know it's not my forte.

When I had to make 70 people redundant at the digital marketing company, it was my manager who took care of it for me.

I slept like a baby because I wasn't personally involved. I received an email every day with a quick report on what happened just because I was curious. The problems were there for him to solve.

If you find that you're getting dragged into all the stuff that you hate in the business, then something is wrong. When you start thinking like an investor, then you let someone else do it because that's their job. Your job is to go and find more companies to buy.

The idea is to merge your ideal lifestyle and your personal skills with the opportunities that you find to create a deal-making strategy that's right for you. It might not happen overnight, but it will become clearer over time.

Once you have the strategy, you will know what type of businesses to buy, and when you know what type of businesses to buy, you know where to go and look for them.

My strategy is to buy and consolidate children's day-care nurseries. I'm particularly interested in this sector. There's so much merger and acquisition activity going on and some huge exit multiples.

Now I know exactly what I'm going for. I know the size of nursery and the geographical location that I'm looking for. I also know that I want nurseries that own a freehold property. That's my criteria. I have a great person who will be running them all for me.

Why choose a profitable business?

If you buy a profitable business, you'll have income from day one and an asset that has a clear value.

You can get the second management tier to run the business for you.

You can also bolt on a profitable business to an existing business. Let's say you have a business with low sales, and then you buy a profitable business that has a stellar sales team. You could use that team to sell your existing products and services.

Buying a profitable business makes it easy to scale up your existing business. You can buy a business that has complementary products or services to your own.

What's more, it will be easier for you to raise cash and borrow against the business. You can always sell shares in the profitable business (provided you have a rock-solid shareholders' agreement in place, of course) or liquidate the assets.

Think about this: if your business is generating something like a monthly £9500 cashflow on top of the £10,000 that you're taking out, then you can go to a bank and get a business loan for £500,000 against that £9500 cashflow. You can invest that £500,000 in property or a savings fund, for example.

Why choose a distressed business?

You can usually buy a distressed business for next to nothing. You can acquire the assets and contracts (whether it's rolling contracts or long-term contracts). These will give you great visibility of future revenue, which makes it an easy purchase.

Theo Paphitus from Dragon's Den made his fortune by never paying more than £1 for a business – they were all distressed purchases.

If you buy the shares of the business from its shareholders, you own the assets and liabilities, which could include bad debts, creditors, long property leases and stock-in-trade. You can avoid this scenario by buying the assets and putting the company into administration as part of the deal. The seller does a simultaneous closure of the old business while you buy the assets. For example, if a supplier calls you three months later and says the old company still owes him £25,000 in unpaid invoices, you aren't the one who has to pay him. The administrator will deal with that.

A friend of mine buys IT companies for the rolling contracts that most of them have. He has one office, and he buys IT companies and consolidates them into his business. All the contracts are serviced by that one business.

Don't think that just because a business is struggling, it is a business that you can't fix – You can. A distressed business can offer huge ROI once you've turned things around by cost-cutting and improving things like marketing and sales.

Earlier this year, I was considering buying a distressed B2B telemarketing company. I wanted it because every business I buy needs marketing, and it would have a readymade client list. The person who bought it was the managing director of the business. I had offered her a 20% shareholding, but the private equity firm that owned the business offered her a better deal. You don't win 'em all.

Liabilities can be managed if the business is distressed. You can put the business through an administrative process, which is a phrase that strikes fear into most owners' hearts because it implies failure. In this world it equals success.

I have a colleague who buys and sells distressed businesses. He only buys businesses that have at least £20m annual revenue. He pays a nominal amount of money upfront, and the business is put into administration, and the assets are moved into a new company. It's the only way to make it work. My friend and dealmakers like him who do this have become multi-millionaires.

Dealmakers make more money than business operators – every time.

Distressed businesses often have scope for cost-cutting and huge ROI. You can't really go wrong if you're doing a £1 distressed deal. Think about it: your financial investment is probably going to be £1. You probably spend more than that every day buying a cup of coffee.

Which sector should you buy a business in?

Choose a sector that matches your skills or interest, or that complements your existing business if you own one and which offers opportunities for growth.

Look for one that has a recurring revenue model. The £4.7m business that I bought for £1 had £3m in annual direct debit payments. That meant I didn't have to go and find new customers every month. It had recurring revenue. That's a great business model.

The business you buy should have good market projection. You should look for sectors with growth potential. Use your common sense and research to establish if this is the case before making a move.

The sector should have barriers to entry for new competitors such as a licence to trade.

The sector should provide you with the opportunity to consolidate. You can become the market leader by consolidating smaller businesses. At the moment, I'm buying day nurseries. One of the reasons I'm investing in this market is because I discovered that the third largest day nursery business in the UK, which had 90 nurseries, sold for £166m last year to an international childcare business. The American publicly listed company now owns more than 300 nurseries in the UK and more than 1,000 worldwide.

Another reason for investing in nurseries is that there are 6,000 individual nurseries in the UK, which gives me plenty of opportunities for consolidation. I'll never run out of nurseries to buy, ever.

I started in the daycare nursery sector with a little bit of marketing; I sent out a 1000 letters to a 1000 nurseries at random. I didn't put the stamps on myself – I got someone else to do it. I received 50 responses. If you're into marketing, you know that a 5% response is pretty good. All of those that responded said they would sell me their nursery. Not one of these nurseries was on the open market.

Why would they sell to me? I'm just an individual. The fact is, they don't want to sell to a big corporate. They want to sell to a person, a guy who's going to have a chat with them over coffee and take the time to understand their business and what they've done with it so far.

I know a chap who's bought 50% shares in over 60 optician practices for £1 each. He intends to improve each practice and then consolidate several into a group. He will then sell the group to a private equity firm. He tells practice owners, 'You'll never sell this business as a single entity, but if you sell me half the business, your half will be worth a lot more than it is now.' His marketing manager is then parachuted in to improve each practice's marketing.

A friend of mine discovered that big private equity firms are buying groups of veterinarian practices. He approaches practice owners who want to sell and says, 'I'd like to put in an offer for your business, but I'm going to tell you the game plan. At some point in the future, I want to sell to a group. I'm going to get a dozen vets and form a group. I'd like you to be one of them, and I'd like you to win on the exit when we sell to the big group.

'We're going to form a group and each practice will share the same branding. We won't change the name of your practice, but on every piece of marketing, it will say that your practice is part of this group. We're going to professionalise your marketing and remove any duplications of costs, so we make the whole group profitable. If there are 12 practices that means there are probably 12 bookkeepers. The group only needs one. If we do this then, as a group, we become more profitable, and then we exit together.'

Obviously, the contractual arrangements are key to this, but vets are ripe for consolidation.

The sector shouldn't be one in which the products or services are commoditised. This allows you to create premium (Gold, Platinum and VIP) versions of the products or services. Commoditisation happens in sectors where people can buy the same product or service from small or large businesses. The only distinguishing factor in commoditised products or services is the price. That's because there is no significant difference in quality or how the product or service is used. Companies in these sectors find it nearly impossible to raise prices because buyers can go elsewhere to buy the same products or services at lower prices. Technology products are commoditised. Price, for products like hard disk drives, monitors, keyboards, surge protectors, memory chips and components of laptops and PCs, is usually the only distinguishing factor between different vendors.

The sector should contain bland competitors so that your business can stand out.

If possible, the product or service should represent an emotive rather than an intellectual or grudge purchase. The grudge purchase is one that gives buyers no pleasure, but is something they must buy (like toilet paper, clothing irons or tyres). Having said that, the turnaround of Scott, the tissue paper company in America, is a success story worth reading.

It should be one in which you understand the customers' point of view. You know the problem they're trying to resolve. That's another reason for investing in day nurseries. I understand the customer's POV because I have a baby daughter who has just started attending a day nursery. I have researched the sector thoroughly, so I understand the trials and tribulations of nursery day care owners.

The sector should be one in which customers are frustrated because no business is offering a solution to their problem. This provides you with enormous scope to swoop in with the ideal solution.

It might be a sector that's run by subject experts rather than business experts. Technical or subject matter experts will be so engrossed in developing the product or service, they'll miss business opportunities that you can spot and leverage.

It might be a sector that has a poor reputation so that customers don't know who to trust. Your revitalised business can stand out by delivering on your promises and providing exemplary customer service.

So, what kind of sectors meet these criteria for consolidation?

- Veterinarian practices
- Opticians
- Children's nurseries
- Accountancy practices
- Chiropractors
- Dental practices
- Spas
- Gyms
- Bookkeepers
- Public Relations agencies
- Advertising agencies
- Marketing agencies

The contractual details of these businesses will be key. You should be able to make huge cost-savings when you consolidate several companies.

What sectors should you avoid (unless you have expertise in them)?

You should avoid any sector that you don't understand. For instance, I avoid anything tech-related because I have absolutely no understanding of it. I went to see someone who ran a business with a retail product. I sat in his office and said, 'Can you explain how this works?' and he did, but I still didn't understand. So he asked his operations manager to explain it to me. It was very confusing: I just didn't get it, and so I said, 'I'm sorry, but if I don't understand this business, I can't spend time on it.'

I would also recommend that you steer clear of the retail sector. It is so competitive that unless you have a background and passion for it, I suggest you look for easier sectors to invest in. There are always exceptions, of course, like Theo Paphitus.

I also recommend that you stay away from highly regulated markets and disrupted markets. I was approached by the owner of a taxi service with hundreds of location-specific taxi websites. It would have been an interesting proposition before Uber entered the market, but now the competition is too tough. I passed on the opportunity.

The challenge with buying a distressed business is that it can take a little time for a seller to admit that it is distressed. They will insist it's a wonderful business.

My advice is to buy a mix of both profitable and distressed businesses. It's all about spreading risk, without investing your own cash.

Your mission

Your mission is to find a sector in which opportunity meets your goals, and in which you can use your skills and knowledge. If possible, it should be a business in which you can do the things you love and are good at, and then delegate the things you dislike to others.

You need to decide whether you want profitable or distressed businesses, or both.

You also need to know what you intend to do with the business once you've bought it. Will you

- Run it for profit?;
- Fix it to sell (and make a profit)?;
- Manage or steer it yourself?;
- Keep it as a standalone business or merge it with another?; or
- Flip it?

Obviously, your decision will depend on your long-term plan, and whether you want to leave a legacy, make an eventual sale, start over once you've sold the business, or retire.

STEP 2
Deal Origination

How do you find deals? You look for business owners who are ready to sell.

A corporate owner or a private equity fund may want to get rid of a business if it hasn't grown as fast as they expected it to.

Or if the business owner wants to retire.

Almost all the phone calls I currently receive are from people who tell me they want to retire, and they don't have an exit plan. They say things like, 'I need to sell soon because I can't do this forever.'

The owner might be drowning in debt or facing a heavy tax bill. I have the same experience with property owners. They'll tell me things like, 'Look, I need this amount of money now to pay off my credit card bills. I'm not concerned about what I sell my property for, as long as I can pay off the mortgage and have some money left over to pay off my debts.'

You're looking for an owner who has lost interest in the business. They have a great business, but they don't want to put any more effort into it.

You're also looking for an owner who is tired. You meet some of these business owners who want to sell; they're knackered, they've had enough, they just want to get out.

Or the owner might have personal reasons for wanting to get out of the business. It might be to do with their health, a desire to spend more time with their partner or children, or because they're going through a divorce or want to move to another country.

A woman I recently spoke with told me she needed to sell her business by the end of the month because that was when the NHS would be stopping her husband's carer. She said, 'I need to be at home with him. I need to do a deal.'

This was a win-win situation: I was able to buy the business for a lot less than it was worth, and she was able to exit and look after her husband. Plus, we structured the deal so that she receives 20% of the business' profits for the next three years. She's delighted with the outcome.

You need to determine what the seller wants from you. You might be surprised to know that money isn't always at the top of a seller's list. Some sellers want peace of mind knowing that their business is in safe hands, and that you'll look after the staff and customers. Be aware that it may not be possible to keep all the staff. You can't always protect jobs. If it's overstaffed, then that's probably where all the money is going.

If it's a distressed business, they might want to hand you the keys and walk away.

Uncover what they want. If you do, you can get a deal done a lot faster. You need to acknowledge what they have done so far. You could say, 'I can see how much hard work and effort you've put into this business. If I take over, I promise that I'm going to put in the same hard work and effort too. I'm not going to drop the ball.'

What motivates people to sell their businesses?

No doubt they set up their company with high hopes of an independent wealthy life. They might be selling for any of the following reasons:

- They're tired, or burnt out from dealing with the pressures of running the business;
- They or someone close to them is ill, and they no longer have the time to dedicate to the business;

- The business didn't live up to their expectations or dreams;
- They want to cash in and retire;
- They want to retrain;
- They want to be an employee – running a business just isn't for them;
- They don't have a family member to pass on the company to;
- They want to relocate and know they can't take the business with them;
- They realise they don't have the skills or expertise to take the business to the next level of growth;
- They have identified another opportunity that interests them more. This is very typical of entrepreneurs who enjoy the set-up phase, but not the scaling-up process; or
- The business is facing a huge tax bill whether it's corporation tax, VAT or PAYE. Don't worry, there are ways of dealing with this.

What does the seller of a profitable business want from you?

It's likely that the business owner will want a lump sum or retirement income so they can, at last, enjoy the fruits of their labour.

They might also want to know that their 'baby' will be safe in your hands, whether that's their staff, customers, suppliers, brand name or reputation. Don't be tempted to make promises you won't be able to keep such as 'Everyone's job is safe.'

Instead, say that you're going to run the business in the best possible way.

What does the seller of a distressed business want from you?

Typically, the owner of a distressed business just wants to be rid of the worry and anxiety. They want to be able to walk away. They may also want to protect their employees' jobs and preserve customer service, if possible.

How to convince people to sell you their business

You need to establish your credibility so that even if you've never bought a business before, the seller will take you seriously. So, set up an investment website. This has to be a standalone website, not a page that you add to the back of another website.

You should also order a set of high-quality business cards with 'Private Investor' and your contact details printed on them.

Focus on your relevant experience. Of course, once you've made your first deal, you'll be able to say that you have experience as a dealmaker. The more deals you make, the more credibility you will have.

You also need to establish rapport with prospective sellers. There are a number of ways to do this. You can begin by preparing an elevator pitch. You need to practice your elevator pitch until it sounds completely natural and can be easily understood.

This is the elevator pitch I use:

'I invest in businesses that have been hit by the recession or where the owner wants to retire or leave. Do you know anyone I should be talking to?'

At the same time, you need to prepare answers for the questions that sellers are likely to ask you. The questions are likely to include:

'Why do you want to buy my business?'
'What do you intend to do with my business?'
'Have you got the funds to buy my business?'

One of the most important attributes of a dealmaker is the ability to ask open-ended questions and listen to the answers. Sellers will reveal a lot about their motivation for selling through those answers.

It's also important to acknowledge the sellers' goals.

Over to you

Once you've chosen a sector that offers you the best potential, decide which kind of seller you'll target. Will it be

- A corporate owner?
- A private equity fund?
- A retiring owner?
- An owner with large debts or facing a huge tax bill?
- A lazy owner?
- A tired owner?
- A frustrated owner? *or*
- An owner who wants to move on to something else (a new business, for example)?

How will you attempt to win over the owner?

Finding businesses for sale

You can either approach a business broker or source the business yourself. Only one in five businesses that are sold are advertised. For that reason, you should take the initiative and seek out prospective sellers rather than relying on finding them through adverts.

Brokers

There are advantages and disadvantages of using a broker to source businesses that are up for sale.

On the plus side, brokers are already working with willing sellers. They're also likely to have comprehensive details about any business that's up for sale. This will speed up the buying process because you won't have to wait while the seller compiles the information you need.

However, there's a risk that the broker will have inflated the seller's expectations in the same way that real estate agents tend to do with property owners. Think back to when you last looked at a property to buy or rent. I bet the agent told you there was a long list of people interested in the property. Business brokers use the same tactic. They, like real estate agents, want to push you into making a bid. You hear there are other people interested in what you want and think, '*Oh my goodness, I've got to make a move really fast.*'

There is also a strong possibility that to get the best price for their client (the seller), they will encourage you to get into a bidding war – whatever you do, don't get involved in a bidding war. Even if you win, you'll have paid more than you should have for the business.

If there's any likelihood of getting involved in a bidding war, I walk away because there are plenty of other businesses to buy.

A broker is also likely to want you to pay 100% of the purchase price at the point of sale.

How else to source businesses for sale

There are plenty of ways to find businesses for sale without resorting to brokers or looking at adverts. They include

- **Word of mouth**
  Talk to your personal and professional network. Your family and friends may know someone who has the kind of business you're interested in. So could your work colleagues or business acquaintances too.

- **Clients**
  Your clients or suppliers may also know people who could be persuaded to sell their business to you. Let them know the kind of business you're interested in and in which sector.

- **Pitching to competitors**
  Arrange meetings with competitors and suggest that your two companies merge. I've used this technique and benefitted from it. How do you approach a competitor? Invite them for

a coffee and say, 'Look, I know we've had our differences over the years, but I've wondered, could we collaborate?'

I say (as if the idea has just popped into my head), 'I wonder what our business would look like if we combined your balance sheet with our balance sheet. Wouldn't that be quite an impressive business?'

It's then that people say things like, 'Well, I'm not sure about that, but I suppose you could buy us if you wanted to.' Then, they follow up with, 'If the price is right.'

By the way, when you hear that phrase 'If the price is right' don't get flustered. Don't think to yourself, 'Oh my God, I've got to go and find millions of pounds from somewhere.'

Instead, just nod and say, 'Absolutely, of course. So, are we saying in principle, you're a willing seller, I'm a willing buyer, and that we could do a deal?'

Then, you need to take immediate action. 'Why don't we have lunch and talk about it now. Let's strike while the iron is still hot.'

This is how you approach your competitors. Do it with enough competitors, and you could start to own your market.

- **Web listings**
  There are online directories that list businesses for sale like **www.rightbiz.co.uk**. Find one that specialises in your chosen sector.

- **Direct Marketing**
  Buy or build a database that contains the names and physical addresses of business owners in the specific sector you're targeting. I recently bought a mailing list of nurseries in England and sent out a direct mail letter to a 1,000 of them. I received more than 50 responses from nursery owners who

had not put their businesses on the open market, but who were interested in selling. What's more, I'm still getting responses to that initial letter months after it was sent.

Write a personal letter. Make sure it doesn't look like marketing. Be respectful and empathetic.

Emphasise that you are a private investor. Business owners are likely to want to sell to an individual than a market leader or established company. Share your motive for wanting to buy businesses in their sector.

The timing of the delivery is critical, so aim to have your letter arrive on Monday mornings. That way your letter will arrive just when they're most in need of an emotional lift!

- **Advertising**
  Place adverts in publications that serve your sector. Your advert can say something like, 'Private investor seeking new business opportunity. Contact [your email] for more information.' A classified ad in one of these publications is likely to be very cheap, but do negotiate on the price. Don't accept the published rate card.

- **Search engine ads**
  Advertise on the major search engines like Google or Bing to attract willing sellers. You'll need to invest in PPC advertising and have a landing page where sellers can enter their contact details.

- **Display ads**
  You can help attract the interest of willing sellers by using Display Ads on platforms such as LinkedIn, Google and Facebook.

- **Organic social media**
  Write brief posts on social media platforms such as LinkedIn, Facebook and Twitter to let your followers, fans and friends

know that you are actively looking for businesses to buy. I put a post on LinkedIn and received 17 responses. Three of those businesses immediately interested me. One or two of those three are going to come off.

- **Trade Shows**
  Visit trade shows that cater to your target sector. Use it as an opportunity to contact business owners. Let them know you're interested in buying profitable or distressed companies and in which sector.

- **Other dealmakers**
  Get to know other dealmakers and let them know the sector you're looking at, and what kind of businesses you're interested in buying.

- **Partnering**
  Form a partnership with another dealmaker. However, to avoid making the same very costly mistake I made, make sure you pay a lawyer to draw up a rock-solid partnership agreement. I don't want you to be left out of pocket like I was.

- **Deal swapping**
  Swap deals with other dealmakers. After all, a deal you don't want might just be someone else's 'dream deal'.

- **Administrators**
  There are a few drawbacks to going through administrators. You won't be able to carry out due diligence on the purchase. So you'll be buying the assets 'sight unseen' and will probably have to provide a blind bid. On the plus side, administrators might agree to staged payments.

STEP 3
Deal or No Deal?

By using one or more of the previous methods of finding deals, you'll undoubtedly be contacted by willing sellers. Now what?

Before you arrange a face-to-face meeting

Call the seller when you're in the right state of mind. The call is your opportunity to find out more about the business and whether the deal is worth pursuing.

During the call, be open about your situation. Explain why you want to buy businesses in the sector. Don't make the seller feel as if you are conducting an interrogation. It should feel like a friendly chat.

Listen to what the owner says to get a better understanding of why they want to sell. Here's the thing, the words they use will reveal what they want.

For example:

- Goals: Your seller will use phrases such as 'retire', 'slow down', 'walk away', 'spend more time with my family'.
- Money: Your seller will reveal what they are looking for by using phrases such as 'regular income', 'lump sum', 'nest egg', 'If someone offers me…'.
- Business: Your seller will describe what they want a new owner to do with the business by using phrases such as 'Look after my staff' or 'A safe pair of hands'.

- Urgency: Your seller will tell you how quickly they want to sell by using phrases such as 'I'm in no rush', 'I'm not going anywhere', or 'I'm looking to close this by…'.

Most sellers will tell you there is a lot of interest in the business. Don't take them at face value. They are hoping you'll panic and raise your price. Remember, there are many businesses for sale, so there's no reason to increase your offer or get into a crazy bidding war.

During the call, find out about the state of the business. Ask for a print out of the bank statements. Business owners will want to give you management accounts, but what you want is bank statements.

The Signs of a Solid Business

A profitable business will have the following:

- High margins: 60% of Gross Profit.
- Sizeable assets: Inventory, property, stock. For example, the company I bought for £1 had 80 unused Apple Macs, which we were able to sell off as a job lot for £40,000. In other words, I made money the day I bought the business.
- Recurring revenues: You need to know there is sufficient revenue to cover:
  - Your £10,000 monthly management fee – or more if the company can afford it.
  - Finance repayments
  - Any deferred payments to seller
- Sufficient funds to cover operating expenditure (OpEx) and capital expenditure (CapEx). Make sure the business has sufficient funds to cover its operating expenses (for example, salaries, rent, insurance, property tax, research and development, pension plan contributions and business travel). It should also have sufficient funds to cover necessary capital expenditure (such as hardware or vehicles).

- Long-standing contracts.
- Substantial IP. These could include trade secrets, copyrights, patented and unpatented products or technology or processes, use rights, licences and so on.
- A history of steady sales. Beware of fast growth in sales because this might require a substantial capital injection to finance growth.
- Automated marketing.
- High performing marketing controls – these will help you attract and convert a steady stream of leads for the business and include:
  - Sales letters;
  - Email sequences;
  - Web pages; and
  - Collateral.
- Streamlined and systemised processes.
- Loyal, trained and qualified staff.
- A 'Can Do' culture.

Signs of a business that can be improved

Whether the business is profitable or distressed, there's usually room for improvement. Be on the lookout for businesses that have

- High revenue, poor profits. These businesses offer plenty of cost-cutting opportunities.
- Poor cash-flow management. You can sometimes solve a business' problems by changing the payment structure. You tell customers, 'I know we used to invoice you, and you paid 90 days later, but now we're moving to a direct debit system where instead of us having to chase your accounts department, the direct debit just kicks in at the end of the month. It's better for everyone that way because you don't get a huge bill every three months.' You immediately improve your company's cash flow.

- Low pricing. These businesses offer you scope to raise prices at once by between 10–15% as well as to create premium options (for example, Silver, Gold and Platinum versions of the product or service).
- Untapped revenue streams. These are the least costly, fastest and most profitable ways to grow business revenue. For example, you could package your business' products and services differently and sell them to a new audience or find complementary products and services that you could sell to the existing customer base. Likewise, you could offer up-sells, down-sells and cross-sells of your products and services to increase sales.
- No marketing. If a company has survived purely on word-of-mouth recommendations, imagine what will happen to sales, turnover and profits when marketing is used consistently.
- Untested marketing. By measuring marketing, it will be possible to determine what does and doesn't work. You can stop unsuccessful marketing campaigns, measure and, therefore, improve all future marketing campaigns.
- Lost customers. You can launch marketing programmes aimed at reactivating lost or dormant clients.
- A database that is sitting idle. If you discover the business has, at some point, collated the contact details of previous and existing customers, but is not using it to drive more sales, you can be sure that you can boost revenue by putting that database to work. If the company's sales are created by a monthly email, make it a weekly one and see sales go up.
- Inefficient procedures. Let's say the company has poor procedures for issuing invoices and that has had a knock-on effect on cash flow. *Late payments affect almost half of all SMEs in the UK. It's so bad that about 50% of SMEs spend up to four hours a week chasing late payments. Some businesses employ someone specifically to chase* outstanding invoices. You can remedy this by introducing procedures to ensure:

-Rigorous credit checks are carried out on prospective new clients.
- Clients sign a contract or agree to T&Cs that specify when they must pay your invoice and late or overdue fees.
- Invoices are issued promptly.
- Clients are offered a range of payment options.
- An invoice tracker system is used that issues alerts when invoices are overdue.
- Invoices are issued on the same date every month.
- Regular weekly or monthly internal finance meetings review invoices.
- Late payment penalties are applied.

- Little use of systems.
- Bloated and overstaffed.
- Low-skilled staff with a willingness to learn.
- Low motivation levels.

Signs of a Problem Business

Some profitable and distressed companies should be avoided because they will be too problematic to run. It's best just to walk away and look for something better. How can you tell which business is problematic?

- Owners with inflated expectations of their business.
- Problem owners.
- Family businesses.
- Sole traders.
- Unpredictable owners who keep changing their mind
- Entrepreneurs with technical assets but no clients.
- Flippers or serial entrepreneurs.
- Businesses with investors. The investors will usually want to reap maximum ROI and loathe writing off their investments.
- Businesses whose successes are based on the value their owners bring to the table. This is typical in smaller businesses, particularly

those in which the owner is directly involved in direct client relationships, consultancy or training. In such cases, the business may suffer once that owner is no longer involved.
- Businesses with multiple owners who can't agree.

Problem circumstances:

- Low revenues;
- Erratic cashflow;
- Limited contracts;
- No assets to liquidate;
- High capex: the money pit. You'll have to keep spending to keep the business afloat;
- Bad reputation; and
- Low-skilled staff with little potential or interest in improving their skill level.

  You'll likely have to spend a great deal of time (or money) on rehiring.

Evaluating the Opportunity

After speaking with the seller and looking closely at the business, you should have a clear idea about:

- The reasons the owner wants to sell.
- The owner's timescale.
- The owner's goals and priorities.
- The owner's valuation and expectations.
- An explanation for numbers that concern you. For example, why sales have dipped in the past 12 months or why, if turnover increased, profits were static or even fell.
- The scope of a deal that suits both of you. Clarify what deal you can construct and explain to the seller that while it won't make him or her a millionaire, but it will help them achieve their non-financial goals.

- Is this an owner who is going to be difficult to deal with or who will drag the process out?

Your next challenge is to value the business and decide how you will fund the deal. Work with the assumption that you won't use your own money. Can you use cash flow to provide deferred payments? You can hire an accountant to help you work out how to do this – but hire the right accountant!

Take a snapshot valuation

How much is the business worth based on its past performance?

Cash and asset valuation

Identify the cash in the business and its sellable assets, so that you can approach a financier with solid numbers.

Projection

What cash will the business generate to cover running costs and liabilities?

What will your exit strategy be? Is there an obvious buyer for this business once you've added value?

Remember, if you don't have the financial expertise to do this evaluation, hire someone to do it on your behalf.

STEP 4
Meeting the Seller

Arrange a face-to-face meeting with the seller at a hotel near the business location so you can walk over and take a look at the company if the meeting goes well.

During the meeting, remember to emphasise the benefits the seller will receive from doing a deal with you. That is, you can make the sale happen quickly, and if the seller deals with you, they will save on broker's fees.

Remember your Unique Selling Proposition – you're a private rather than corporate investor.

Be keen, but not too keen. Make it clear that you love a challenge. Don't give the seller the impression that you're desperate, or that you will pay any price for the business.

Take a problem-solver approach.

Do use your coaching and listening skills. For example, use open-ended questions (those that require more than a 'Yes' or 'No' response). You could ask the seller:

'How can I help you?'
'What's important to you?'
'How do you see the deal working?'
'What does a solution look like?'
'What's your timescale?'

Don't be afraid to be direct. So ask a question like, 'Is it all about the money for you?'

You should also find out:

- The history of the company;
- What are the revenue and profits for its products or services?;
- What is the seller's background?;
- What is the seller's area of expertise?;
- What is the seller's salary and other financial benefits or perks?;
- Will the seller be available to act as a consultant to the business?;
- Why hasn't the business expanded further?;
- Who are its main market competitors?;
- What are the key trade publications, tradeshows and websites?;
- What do customers like best about the company's products or services?;
- Why do customers buy its products or use its services?; and
- Does the business have a customer who is responsible for more than 10% of the purchases? This could indicate a business with an over-reliance on one major customer. What would happen to the business if that one client takes their business elsewhere?

During this, or a subsequent meeting (or later in the buying process), you will ask them to sign a Non-Disclosure Agreement (NDA). It will restrain you from revealing or sharing the information that the seller provides during the sales process.

It's designed to protect business-sensitive information such as customer contracts, and financial statements that the seller will have to disclose during the sale process. If this information falls into the wrong hands, it could damage the business' reputation and potential earnings. If suppliers or clients discovered the company was in financial trouble, for instance, they might cancel contracts. Likewise, if one of its competitors was to discover that key supplier or customer contracts were up for renewal, there is a possibility they could swoop in to poach the business.

The seller will also want to ensure that employees aren't aware the business is up for sale.

Make a Site Visit

Visiting the business premises not only gives you the opportunity to see things for yourself and to learn more, but also to address the business owner's anxieties about the sale. The business owner will worry that you intend to:

- Make radical changes to the business that will affect the brand, customer service and its reputation.
- Asset strip the business
- Make widespread layoffs.

Don't make any promises. Just state that you will try to do your very best for the business. You can reassure them by saying something like, 'In time, I'll want to put my stamp on things, but I don't know what that is yet.'

You're there to listen and observe and not to demonstrate how much cleverer you are than the business owner. Don't ask confrontational questions because you'll just make the owner feel defensive and bullied. Be diplomatic. Instead of asking, 'Why are you employing him?' ask, 'What is his role in the business?'. Rather than asking, 'Why did you do *that*?' ask, 'What was the thinking behind that?'.

Keep quiet about how you intend to improve the business. Why? – Because your prospective seller might just take the business off the market and try doing what you intended to do.

STEP 5

Crafting Your Offer

Your offer will depend on your goals, the state of the business and what the seller wants. Hence, your offer for a distressed business will be very different from that for a profitable business or one that's in administration.

Your distressed business offer

As the prospective buyer of a distressed business, you're the answer to the seller's prayers. You are the person who is going to allow them to walk away from the fire. For that reason, you're not going to pay them for the privilege. It's £1 or nothing!

You have two choices – you can buy the shares, or buy the assets.

If you buy the shares, you'll own everything, including all the bad things such as:

- Debts including creditors, pending invoices and HMRC tax bills; and
- Liabilities including property leases, software, staff on fixed contracts, pensions, and so on.

Avoid buying the shares in the company!

If you buy the assets, you'll only own the good things such as:

- Property;
- Stock;

- Inventory;
- IP;
- Customer contracts. If you buy the company, write to the customers to explain a different business will invoice them in the future;
- Website and website content;
- Orders;
- Transferable contracts;
- Database;
- Customer lists;
- Trade names and marks;
- Logos and service marks;
- Domain names;
- Procedural manuals;
- Supplier or referral lists;
- Patented and unpatented products, technology or processes;
- Use rights;
- Licences; and
- Advertising content.

Your offer for the assets of a business in administration

There are several downsides to making an offer on the assets of a business that is in administration. For starters, you won't have the opportunity to meet with managers and get to know the business. Then, there's the likelihood that other buyers are interested, so you could find yourself embroiled in a bidding war. Third, administrators tend to want to make a rapid deal, so you have to act fast!

The best strategy is to bid on assets that will complement your current business. Put in low, manageable offers. Pay over time if possible, with the first payment sufficient to cover the administrator's fee!

Your offer for a profitable business

If you have to pay something for the business, don't risk your own money. Remember, your bank balance is designed to grow not shrink!

You need to protect your cash. Don't give it all away at once. Aim for staggered payments (called 'Deferred Consideration'). Even though you'll be using someone else's money, you can't be too generous. When you're crafting an offer, keep the negative aspects of the business top of mind.

You could offer to:

- Pay the asking price in stages;
- Pay a negotiated price immediately; and
- Make a small initial payment with the balance deferred.

Let's say you're making an offer on business with a £24k asking price.

You could pay £24k over time. That might be £1k per month over two years, or £2k per month over 12 months, but with a three-month delay on the first payment.

Or,

You could pay a negotiated price immediately so paying £18k today (or within 30 days) to conclude the deal.

Or,

You could make a small initial payment with the balance deferred. So you could pay £6k to cover the first six months in advance; then, from Month 7 pay £1k per month for 18 months.

STEP 6
Clever Financing

How to fund the acquisition

If you agree to pay money on completion, it has to come from somewhere, and it should come from anywhere but your own bank account! That leaves you with two ways of funding your purchase – either find ways to access finance or release cash from the business.

Access Finance

- **Vendor finance**
  This is a form of lending in which a company lends money to the borrower to buy the vendor's products or property. Vendor finance is usually in the form of deferred loans from, or shares subscribed by, the vendor.

- **Asset-based finance**
  Asset-based lending is a business loan secured by assets. The loan, or line of credit, is secured by inventory, accounts receivable and/or other balance-sheet assets.

- **Cashflow Finance**
  With cashflow financing, the loan is backed by the company's future cash flow. The repayments are based on projected future cashflow too.

- **Credit Card Advance**
  If the business accepts credit card payments and has been active in the past six months, you can borrow cash from an advance company against future credit card sales. The provider will probably take a portion of your daily credit card sales until the entire amount has been repaid.

- **Business Overdraft**
  You use the business' overdraft to fund your acquisition

- **PayPal Working Capital**
  If the business has had a PayPal Business or Premier account for at least three months and processes at least £12k in PayPal sales annually, you may be able to arrange a merchant cash advance. Repayments are automatically deducted from the PayPal account as a percentage of each sale until the cash advance amount and fixed fee are paid in full. You can also make additional repayments or even pay the cash advance in full without additional charges.

- **Private Investors**
  You could find other private investors to loan you the money to fund the deal.

Moving towards the deal

Decision in Principle (DIP)

This gives you provisional go-ahead subject to start Due Diligence. It means you can make your offer with confidence and know exactly what and how to negotiate.

The Offer

- Explain your deal structure.
- Tease out objections.
- Revise the offer, but don't throw away concessions.

- Negotiate a deal that works for you both.
- Agree to Head of Terms.
- Summary terms to give you a period of exclusivity and take the deal into Due Diligence.
- Aim to complete negotiations first, so this represents the final deal; however, be ready to renegotiate since Due Diligence often brings skeletons out of the closet.

STEP 7
Due Diligence

This is the method by which you get access to all the company's files, records, information and personnel to confirm that everything you've been told by the seller is accurate. It also helps determine that it is worth the price you're being asked to pay, and that it's free from contingent or unknown liabilities and is capable of continuing to trade.

It pays to have several deals bubbling at the same time rather than just one. That's because the Due Diligence process is often long. It's also the point at which deals fall through. It often changes the deal because you discover things that the seller might have hidden or glossed over.

Sellers and brokers will pressure you to conduct the Due Diligence quickly, but don't be rushed. You'll probably need at least 20 business days to carry out a thorough investigation.

It's generally carried out in the following three areas:

- Legal due diligence (carried out by your solicitors). A request is sent to the seller's solicitors for information and documentation. Eventually, your solicitors will prepare a legal due diligence report for you. It will explain the legal position of the business and areas of concern, and it will provide recommendations that you may need to address post completion.
- Financial and tax due diligence (carried out by your accountants).
- Commercial due diligence (carried out by you or an advisor).

The Due Diligence will investigate the following aspects of the company:

Ownership of Assets

- Website and domain;
- Trademarks and Intellectual Property (IP);
- Marketing materials;
- Customer contracts;
- Database; and
- Owned premises.

Warranties

- Non-Disclosure Agreement (NDA);
- Non-Compete Clauses;
- Debentures; and
- Risk scenarios and level of protection.

Liabilities

- Creditors;
- Historic debt;
- Looming payments (especially HMRC); and
- Long-term contracts including vehicles and leased premises.

Shareholders' Agreements (if you aren't the only new owner and have a partner) reflecting

- Investment capital;
- Sweat equity ; and
- Exit terms.

STEP 8
Closing the Deal

You need an expert team consisting of an accountant and a lawyer who specialise in mergers and acquisitions and taxation.

Preparing for the deal

Set up a Special Purchase Vehicle (SPV).

Get the right legal structure so that you pay the right amount of tax and not a penny more.

Prepare to take control of the bank accounts, especially with distressed companies. Make sure all the necessary documents are ready to be presented to the right person at the bank the moment you take over.

Prepare your staff announcement. You can tell employees that things are going to get better.

Get your external accountant ready.

Create an action plan for your first 100 days after you sign the deal. It's important to do it before the actual sale is done – you don't want to be caught out.

Your Action Plan for a Distressed Business

Develop a full plan before you take ownership:

- Detail the spending cuts you'll initiate for immediate cost savings.

- Decide how many layoffs you'll need to make.
- Plan your negotiations with creditors.
- Find out how much wriggle room you have regarding contracts.
- Launch it on Day One.

Your Action Plan for a Profitable Business

Sketch out the options you have and any ideas for:

- New products or services;
- New marketing campaigns;
- Staff training needs; and
- Detail your first objectives.

Protecting the Deal

- Risk of deal fatigue.
- Seller's remorse.
- Buyer's frustration.

STEP 9
Taking Ownership

Your top priorities.

In the first 24 Hours, ensure that you do the following:

- Take control of the bank account and keep a rein on spending;
- Hand-deliver your letter of ownership to the bank;
- Restrict purchase authority;
- Destroy credit cards;
- Change all bank passwords;
- Freeze all invoice payments;
- Cancel all direct debits; and
- If the business is distressed, initiate redundancies.

In the first 100 Days:

- Review expenditure line by line;
- Identify new revenue streams;
- Review staffing requirements;
- Change computer passwords;
- Seed the client/prospect database;
- Offload saleable assets;
- Seek a rent holiday. You can often get a three-month rent holiday;
- Renegotiate long-term contracts; and
- Approach potential buyers.

Getting people on side

Your Staff

As the new owner, you should be:

- Pleasant;
- Approachable;
- Open;
- Accommodating;
- Willing to listen; but
- NOT too friendly.

Earn their trust and let them tell you what the seller withheld!

Your Creditors

- Prioritise urgent cases. Stopping payments will unearth the 'squeaky wheels'.
- Show willingness to pay, by renegotiating terms.
- Make it clear that you want to fix the mess you inherited.
- You're not the 'bad guy'.

STEP 10

Fixing the Business

It's always easier to improve someone else's work than to build something from scratch.

Cut all unnecessary costs.

Quick Wins

- Negotiate payment holidays.
- Escape from oppressive contracts.
- Conduct an 80:20 review of the business and eliminate:
  - Unprofitable products and services;
  - Unnecessary job roles;
  - Under-performing staff; and
  - Unmeasured/low value marketing.
- Sell unwanted stock/inventory.
- Introduce an austerity drive. Review employee perks, company vehicles, and so on.

Long-Term Gains

- Merge with another business – if you own or can buy one.
- Recruit or train staff to bring external functions in-house.
- Measure all your marketing and focus the budget on high performers.

Cultural Change

You have to decide what will happen to the staff at your new business. Will you:

- Retain and develop the employees?
- Make employees redundant?

If you decide to make an employee redundant, it's imperative that you act immediately and with absolute professionalism. Pay everything that's owed and ensure they are off the premises as quickly as possible.

Instant growth

- Increase your prices by 10% – most business owners under charge or get stuck with historic pricing;
- Offer Silver, Gold and Platinum tiers of your products or services;
- Reactivate lost customers;
- Call your best customers with an upgrade offer;
- Ask for referrals;
- Cross-sell products between your two businesses;
- Get endorsed by a business associate;
- Add a retention deal;
- Launch a new offer;
- Run an event, with an on-the-day promotion;
- Add an offer to a customer mailing;
- Start sending regular emails;
- Follow up with your pending orders; and
- Sell or swap your lost leads with a friendly competitor.

Long-Term Growth

Create a solid business

- Launch a new product or service;
- Write a book or shoot a video and use to expand your mailing list;

- Run marketing split tests and find the perfect messages;
- Run an 80:20 audit to determine your top customers then focus most of your marketing spend on attracting people like them. If you can focus more of your efforts on the 20% of your best customers and less on the 80% high maintenance customers, you'll increase your profitability;
- Split your mailing list into segments and create relevant offers for each of them;
- Identify new markets. Find out who else will want or need your products or services;
- Find bulk-deal opportunities;
- Create a reseller network;
- Create an affiliate system;
- Create a loyalty programme, adding goodwill and 'pain of disconnect';
- Model the performance of your top salespeople; and
- Forge a joint venture with a related business.

And crucially build an automated funnel to bring in qualified leads. Although a large number of prospects enter the widest part of the funnel (for example, land on your website or see your newspaper advertisement), only a fraction of those people will end up buying from you. An even smaller amount of those who buy from you will love your service so much that they'll become your 'evangelists', happy to tell everyone they know about your professional services.

A consumer or buyer is likely to go through the following stages during the 'sales journey':

- An awareness phase in which they discover a possible solution to their problem;
- An interested phase in which they conduct some research into a product or service;
- An evaluation phase in which they compare competitors' solutions;

- A decision phase in which a final decision is made; and
- A purchase phase in which they buy your products or retain your services.

The time between awareness and purchase will vary depending upon the urgency of the prospective customer's or buyer's need, and the value of the product or service they're considering. For B2B, the purchasing decision is likely to involve more than one person or department and so, will inevitably take far longer than a B2C decision.

So while the 'sales journey' for a consumer about a low-ticket item, such as a printer cartridge, might be measured in minutes or hours, a B2B 'sales journey' for a high-priced product or complex service might span months or even years.

When you understand the different stages your prospective buyers move through, you'll know what you need to do to help encourage them to proceed to the next level, whether it's making follow-up phone calls, sending them white papers or links to positive reviews of your professional services.

That's why having a marketing funnel is so essential to your success. If you don't know the thought processes that your prospects go through before making a purchase decision, you can't give them exactly what they want, when they want it.

Worse, you're likely to deter rather than encourage their progress. For example, if you bombard first-time visitors to your website with details of how to retain your services on a monthly basis, they're likely to consider it 'too much, too soon' and abandon your site without taking any action at all. However, if you offer those same visitors the opportunity to take an action they consider low-risk, like watch a short video or download a free report that contains information they'll find useful and relevant, they'll be more likely to stick around.

Once you have their contact details, you can continue providing them with the information they want or need, depending on where they are in the sales cycle. From there, you can nurture them through the rest of the sales journey.

Build a Marketing System

Marketing is the strategy you use to attract, convert and keep customers. It's highly likely that the business you buy needs better marketing, even if it's profitable. If it's a distressed company, it probably desperately needs better marketing.

To ensure your marketing brings in a steady stream of high-quality prospects, you need to use more than one tactic (such as email marketing or Facebook advertising). Most businesses rely on three ways of bringing in new business:

- A website;
- Networking; and
- Referrals and repeat business.

Unfortunately, most websites fail when it comes to converting visitors into prospective leads. Networking is time consuming, and referrals only contribute 'organic' growth. If you want to accelerate the business' growth, you need a systematic approach to generating leads and converting them into clients or customers.

Just using one tactic leaves the business vulnerable, since that one tactic might not work in your sector, or it could lose its effectiveness. You need to use an automated marketing system with multiple tactics that work on the business' behalf 24/7 to bring in leads and convert them into loyal paying customers or clients.

Begin by identifying your target market. If your prospective buyers are consumers, identify their age, sex, income, geography and where you can reach them with your marketing message. If your prospective buyers are businesses, identify them in terms of size and location.

Understand the problems your prospective buyers want to solve and then design your marketing messages to capture their attention.

Here are some of the marketing tactics you should consider using in your new business.

Overhaul the website

First-time website visitors spend a few seconds deciding whether it contains what they're looking for. If they can't see what they want in those first few seconds, they will leave and are unlikely to ever return. That's why the layout and content of the website's homepage are so important.

Use videos on your website

Only 20% of the visitors who land on a website will read the text, whereas 80% of them will watch the same content on the same website in video form. What's more, visitors who watch a video on a website stay two minutes longer than average and are 64% more likely to make a purchase.

Use an email marketing system

Email marketing is a cheap yet highly effective marketing tool. You can use email to respond immediately to prospective customers' request for information. You can: contact old clients; communicate with your existing clients; distribute press releases; invite prospective customers to visit your website; and alert prospects and clients alike about new services, sales, discounts, seminars, and special events.

Use the services of an email marketing service provider (such as InfusionSoft, MailChimp, or Aweber) to ensure your emails look professional and are delivered to all your subscribers.

Create an email autoresponder series

With an email autoresponder series, people who sign up to receive your emails are automatically sent a series of emails over a scheduled period. This helps build a relationship between you and prospective customers so that when they're ready to make a purchase, it's your company that springs to mind.

Each email needs to contain information that your prospective and existing customers consider to be useful, informative and relevant.

You should include offers of discounts, great deals and enticing benefits in your autoresponder series too, but you need to do it in a way that doesn't seem like an aggressive sales pitch.

Once you've created an autoresponder series, you can use it repeatedly to convert each new prospect. That leaves you free to work on other areas of your business.

Create a free offer or giveaway

Most visitors to a website arrive looking for information. You can capture their interest and begin converting those 'just browsing' information-hunters into paying customers, if you offer them an enticement such as a piece of free content that answers their questions or solves one of their most pressing problems.

You should insist your visitors give you their email contact details in return for the free report. Once you have your visitors' contact details, you can contact them after they've left your website and begin to develop a relationship with them. You will be able to demonstrate your expertise, reliability and credibility to those visitors so that when they are ready to buy, your company is the one they think of.

Use Facebook marketing

You need to be where your target audience is, and it's more than likely that they'll spend most of their time on social media platforms like Facebook, Google+, YouTube, Instagram, Twitter and LinkedIn. That means you need a presence on those platforms too.

Find out where your customers and prospects are having conversations and where your business can add value.

Use Google AdWords

Google AdWords is a very powerful and fast way to drive visitors to your website.

The trick with AdWords (a type of Pay-Per-Click advertising) is to manage every campaign very carefully.

A poorly managed campaign can cost more than it brings in, but a well-managed one can keep your shop or company in business.

AdWords allows you to reach the people who are looking for what you sell at the moment they're looking and then getting them to respond. To do that, you need to understand your audience and design your message accordingly. You also need to keep testing and refining your message.

Use Remarketing

Remarketing (also known as 'retargeting') is a way of following up with visitors who didn't take any desired action (convert) the first time they visited your website.

Remarketing works by keeping track of people who visit your site and displaying your remarketing ads to them as they visit other sites online.

It generates greater online sales by keeping your brand front and centre and bringing 'window shoppers' back when they're ready to buy. Every time your prospective customer sees your remarketing ads, your brand gains traction and more recognition. The high click-through rates and increased conversions that are typical with remarketing campaigns underscore the value of good branding and repeated exposure.

STEP 11

Building your Portfolio Toward Financial Freedom

Look for synergistic companies. That means:

- Businesses in the same sector;
- Businesses in complementary sectors;
- Businesses where the customers are the same for each company;
- Businesses that are geographically close;
- Businesses that have selling mechanism (for example, they are all online businesses); and
- Business that can share operations and facilities.

Keep streamlining your businesses and selling.

- Streamline all operations;
- Share premises;
- Share facilities;
- Consolidate job roles;
- Consolidate inventory and sell unwanted items; and
- Use your increased buying power to cut better deals.

Selling

- Sell unwanted stock;
- Merge databases to cross-sell products and services;
- Use email marketing for 'quick win' sales;

- Transfer marketing expertise between companies; and
- Share salespeople and facilities.

STEP 12
Exiting – The Big Money Pay Days

When is the best time to sell your business? It's when you have multiple businesses, each making you a consultancy fee of at least £10k a month and they're running well without you, and you're offered the right deal and are happy to walk away.

What's the worst time to sell a business? It's when you **have** to sell – when the business is failing, or you're struggling, and it's affecting your health. You're desperate, and that can only weaken your position.

Most people only have one business, and they are under pressure to sell. They won't get the best price. As a dealmaker, you are in a stronger position as you own several companies.

Get an independent valuation

By getting an accredited firm to conduct an independent and thorough valuation of your business, you'll be in a much stronger position when it comes to negotiating the best price for your business. That's because the valuation will be based on facts rather than wishful thinking.

You can negotiate knowing that the business valuation is based on statistics, sales figures, stock and realistic projections, which makes it more likely that you'll receive a price you're happy with.

Moreover, you'll avoid the likelihood of undervaluing your business and losing out on potential sale earnings. You'll also avoid losing credibility by overvaluing the business.

Flipping from being a buyer to a seller

- As a buyer, you value by adding cash and assets then adjusting for the negatives. As a seller, you value the same way, but adjust for positives.
- As a buyer, you want deferred consideration, but as a seller, you want cash up front.
- As a buyer, you want a contingent option, so payments are performance linked. As a seller, you don't want future payments that are threatened by performance.
- As a buyer, you want the freedom to buy the business with minimum baggage. As a seller, you want to sell everything.
- As a buyer, you don't want personal liability. As a seller, you want a personal guarantee for any future payments.
- As a buyer, you want exclusivity after signing Heads of Terms, but as a seller, you want an 'open contest' where rival buyers race to the finish line.

Selling through a broker

In an ideal world, a broker will:

- Help you reach a realistic valuation;
- Produce an Information Memorandum (IM);
- Find interested buyers through marketing and their own database;
- Field enquiries and offers;
- Guide you through the complex process, from offer to sale;
- Get you maximum value with the terms you ask for; and
- Protect you from restrictive small print.

That doesn't always happen. So how can you be sure the broker you hire will deliver an outstanding service? Talk to other dealmakers and ask for recommendations. Check references/testimonials on the broker's website.

Whatever you do, don't give them free rein – you should monitor all their activity. They are the business equivalent of estate agents.

Selling the business yourself

What will a buyer want to know about your business?

- Financials;
- Intellectual Property;
- Market share;
- Brand reputation;
- Customer lists;
- Supply chains;
- Employees;
- Location;
- Scalability; and
- Market trends.

What are buyers looking for?

- Profits;
- Growth prospects;
- A 'fair price';
- Impressive financial records;
- Motivated skilled employees;
- Good track record;
- Great location; and
- A business that's well known and fun to own.

Research Your Buyer

Before you dive into any negotiations, you'll want to make sure you are prepared.

What to ask potential buyers

- What are their full contact details (assumng contact is made with you by phone, get this information right at the start of the call)?
- What is their business history? Find out what businesses the prospective buyer owns or has owned.

- How do they intend to finance the purchase?
- What minimum monthly income are they hoping to get from the business?
- What is their timeframe for completion?
- Why have they chosen your business?
- What expectations do they have for the handover?
- What changes do they plan to make?
- Will they keep existing staff and clients?

How to prepare for the sale

To make the sale process as smooth as possible, gather all the information that prospective buyers will want to see, including financials, paperwork, legal documents and contracts.

The more organised you appear, the more confidence prospective buyers will have in you and the business.

What documents do you need?

Prospective buyers will want to see paper-based evidence that your claims about the value of your business based on profit and loss figures, assets, contracts and other details are accurate.

Financials

To gauge the level that the business is operating at, how profitable it is and whether it has debts, prospective buyers will want to see financial figures including profit and loss accounts from the past three years as well as up-to-date balance sheets.

Assets

You'll need to prepare a written list of all the business' assets including properties, equipment, IT systems, vehicles, and so on.

Contracts

You'll also need to provide a list of contracts for clients, employees, suppliers and contractors.

Key processes

If the business' success is due to outstanding systems, describe them.

Information Memorandum

An information memorandum is a comprehensive document that is created to highlight ALL of the vital information required for the sale of your business. This document will be shown to prospective buyers after they have reviewed a summary sheet and have signed a confidentiality agreement.

It must be appealing to prospective buyers yet factually accurate, clear and concise.

How to present your business to potential buyers

Once you've had your business valued and prepared all the necessary paperwork along with an NDA, it's time to decide how to present your business to prospective buyers. The more polished and persuasive your presentation, the more excited buyers are likely to be.

It might seem counterintuitive, but it's best to admit the business' weaknesses in your presentation. This will not only save everyone's time, but also demonstrate to prospective buyers your willingness to be honest and transparent. If someone is seriously interested in your business, they will undertake their own investigation and uncover such weaknesses anyway. If you're tempted to gloss over or even hide these weaknesses, the prospective buyer will likely lose faith in you and the deal.

The presentation process

Single page overview detailing main points

This concise document is intended to provide a basic snapshot of your business. Its purpose is to create interest from prospective buyers. The information it should cover includes the following:

- Company name;
- Business sector;
- Unique Selling Point/market differentiator;
- A brief description of your company, its values, achievements, market placement and so on;
- Business structure; and
- NEVER suggest an 'asking price'.

Information Memorandum

This is like a CV for your company and should provide detailed information about the business structure, processes and finances. It should include:

- Financial overview;
- Sales figures;
- Past three years' accounts;
- Financial projections;
- Company history;
- Staff members;
- Client types;
- Products and services;
- Market niche;
- Current opportunity and reason for sale;
- Price and terms of the company's products and services;
- Certifications and licences;
- Physical assets and IP;
- Organisational chart; and
- New products or services.

Meeting the prospective buyers

Do explain your reason for selling. 'Ready for a new challenge' makes a lot of sense if you are unsure of what to say.

Do get professional help

To ensure you get the best deal for your business, don't try to manage the sales process yourself. Hire an M&A lawyer and an accountant. They will help ensure you don't make costly mistakes.

Now... Take Action

The only way you are going to enter the exciting and financially rewarding world of dealmaking is by taking action – Now. Don't put it off for another day, another week, another month or even another year.

Here's the thing, 50% of people will read a book or attend a seminar, feel excited about the content and then do nothing. And 40% of them will be filled with good intentions. They'll tell everyone they know about all the things they're going to do, and then they will do nothing. Only 10% of the people who read a book or attend a seminar will use the information to take action. I want you to be part of the 10%.

To help you, I'm going to give you a 50-point action plan that you should initiate immediately. It has all the steps you need to find a distressed or profitable business and what actions you need to take.

Your 50-Point Action Plan for Wealth

1. Set your goals for the years ahead. Decide what you want regarding your:
   - Lifestyle;
   - Work life; and
   - Money
2. Decide which dealmaking strategy is right for you.

3. Choose a sector for your first acquisition. Decide whether you're going to buy a business in your sector, related sector or an unrelated sector.
4. Choose the financial state of the business that you will buy. Decide whether you'll buy a profitable but improvable, distressed or a highly profitable business.
5. Choose a strategy. Will you:

- Run your business for revenue?
- Fix and flip the business?
- Fix and take revenue then flip?

You'll also need to decide whether you will merge your business ventures.

6. Create your dealmaker website.
7. Order business cards.
8. Perfect your dealmaker elevator pitch.
9. Find a motivated seller with a business that ticks your boxes.
10. Speak to the seller.
11. Sign an NDA.
12. Meet the seller in person.
13. Submit an Information Request.
14. Review the business accounts.
15. Create your offer.
16. Negotiate with the seller.
17. Structure the final deal.
18. Sign Heads of Terms.
19. Enter the Exclusivity Period.
20. Begin Due Diligence and Legals.
21. Renegotiate, if needed.
22. Plan your first 100 days.
23. Close the deal.
24. Take ownership.
25. Take control of the finances.
26. Protect your new assets.
27. Review expenditure and streamline.

28. Renegotiate terms with suppliers.
29. Strike a deal with creditors.
30. Review staffing requirements. Decide if you need to reduce staffing levels or reshuffle personnel.
31. Systemise the business.
32. Offload saleable assets.
33. Make instant sales via 'quick wins'.
34. Identify new products or services. Focus on those that will provide recurring revenue.
35. Identify new markets.
36. Identify new sales channels.
37. Build a robust marketing system. Ensure that you measure performance and incorporate continuous improvement.
38. Expand and segment your email list.
39. Approach prospective buyers.
40. Reduce reliance on contractors.
41. Optimise your sales message and process.
42. Build an empire of complementary businesses.
43. Share people and expertise between your businesses.
44. Share space and facilities.
45. Merge databases and cross-sell.
46. Leverage your increased buying power to negotiate better deals with suppliers.
47. Choose when to exit.
48. Instruct a broker:

- Create an Info Memorandum;
- Help them find buyers;
- Secure finance for the new owner; and
- Monitor the broker's performance.

49. Close the deal. Enjoy your payday!
50. Do it all again!

What can stand in your way?

Many obstacles can get in the way of you doing your first deal. They include:

- Getting started;
- A lack of confidence;
- Fear of failure;
- Motivational dips;
- Changing priorities;
- Time hijackers; and
- Lack of marketing knowledge.

You'll notice that each of these obstacles is related to your thinking. That means you can eliminate them by changing your thinking. Only you can stop procrastinating, feel more confident, stop being afraid, feel motivated, prioritise what's important, manage your time and learn whatever you need. It's all entirely possible.

So, change your thinking and use the information in this book and go for it! You have the information you need to make your first deal.

Join our Mastermind Programme

'If I have seen further it is by standing on the shoulders of giants.'
Sir Isaac Newton

Starting out as a Dealmaker? You're invited to join

Jonathan Jay's *First Ever* Dealmaker's Mastermind

No-one can do this alone! But with a support network, you can:

- ✓ Buy a multi-million pound business, without spending your own money
- ✓ Find, Fund, Fix & Flip the business in less than a year
- ✓ Pay yourself an extra £10k every month – per deal
- ✓ Sell up, and enjoy the biggest payday of your life
- ✓ Share the journey with fellow dealmakers
- ✓ Access a panel of industry experts
- ✓ Stay focused, stay accountable
- ✓ AND become Jonathan's next business partner

JOIN THE DEALMAKER'S MASTERMIND GROUP

Buying and selling businesses will make you much more money than building a business from scratch. Or working for someone else. Or investing in stocks and shares, or property.

It's the fastest route I know of to extraordinary wealth, provided you know exactly what you're doing and that you have the right people around you.

I know deal making is the answer, but I also know there are pitfalls such as putting in the wrong offer, hiring the wrong solicitor or missing the small print in a finance deal. Mistakes like these can quickly make a good deal go bad.

I know this from experience. I've seen deals turn sour in front of my eyes. And I've counted the cost.

If you're starting out as a dealmaker, frankly, you cannot afford to go into it alone. Unless of course you <u>want</u> all the trauma, all the sleepless nights, which I had back in those early days.

You need experts behind you, to steer you through every step of the deal. From finding the business to buy, securing the finances and brokering the deal right through to fixing up the business, and selling it for a payday that is going to make your eyes water.

You need that support.

That's why I'm putting together an exclusive Dealmaker's Mastermind group. It's the first of its kind, anywhere in the UK. It's going to be a roomful of motivated, enthusiastic dealmakers working together alongside a full panel of experts.

If you're in the room, we're all going to work with you as you make your first deal and make it profitable in the span of a year. You'll buy your first business then improve it, so you'll have the choice of selling it for a healthy profit, or keeping it running to enjoy income every month.

At the monthly meetings, you'll get advanced learning, problem-solving and implementation – with easy, proven techniques that you can immediately use. For example, at our first meeting, I'll show you a neat way to find sellers. It's a simple method that can bring you qualified leads within an hour. I want you to leap out of the starting blocks, so your first deal can be lined up before you head home!

Then, as we progress…

We'll role-play buyer-seller scenarios, so you can learn by doing.

I'll bring in guest presenters who'll go deep into vital topics like selling yourself, handling tax and building rapport with buyers.

PLUS, I'll set assignments. Milestones you complete – like advertising to sellers, holding meetings and making offers.

Then there will be the hotseats where you'll share your challenges, and let the group find the answers with the help of my Dream Team, who'll weigh in with their expertise.

You'll get fantastic ideas. You'll commit to action. And make no mistake – you'll be held accountable.

Because we can only help you do this, if you'll follow through.

And remember, we'll be doing business in the room. That deal you don't want? Bring it along. Pass it on to another member. That deal you can't do alone? Find a partner. Co-invest. And you'll get to know other members – what they sell, what they need. So, there'll be a lot of business changing hands.

As a member, you'll have the chance to become my business partner. I'm a compulsive dealmaker, and I'm always looking for that next opportunity, but only with the right people. I've decided that I'm only going to partner with fellow Mastermind members. Because we're the ones who really know what to do. We've got a system. So, we can efficiently do deals, and we can share in some big, fast profits.

Of course, partnering with me is not obligatory! You'll have the skills and confidence to do it alone. But with the right deal, there is the option to co-invest.

There's more to the Mastermind Group, of course, like all the advanced learning you'll get when you're locked in a room with me. And there's my Dream Team, who can help you through all the specialist stuff like financing, creating and getting contracts and marketing the businesses you buy.

They can help you with all of that, because they're the best of the best. They're people I've found through years of searching and painful trial and error. They'll be there in the room when we meet, pitching in with ideas. And they'll be available to you, if you want to work with them one-on-one.

Being part of the Mastermind Group will remove the guesswork. You won't have to cross your fingers and hope you've got things right. Instead, you'll have a team of experts on hand to guide you every step of the way.

And that will remove the risk of losing momentum. Go into it alone, and you could easily get dragged back into your daily work life and put dealmaking on hold. You might let big deals slip through your fingers. But we won't allow that to happen. We'll keep you focused, and we'll motivate you through the hard times.

That's what this Mastermind is – a team of allies who will be with you from the beginning to the end.

The first members are already in and waiting. So there's no time to waste. Act now to get your dealmaking life off the ground, and secure a better future for you and your family.

By this time next year, you'll be profiting from at least one smart, new acquisition. You'll have:

- ✓ Found your first business to buy;
- ✓ Brokered a deal;
- ✓ Raised finance (with zero personal risk);
- ✓ Managed due diligence and taken the deal over the finish line;
- ✓ Analysed your new business and found the leaks;
- ✓ Discovered untapped profits;
- ✓ Built a marketing system that brings in regular leads on autopilot; and
- ✓ Paid yourself a management fee of at least £10k a month

Exclusive Access to My Dream Team

You'll have access to my Dream Team. This might be my most closely guarded secret – my inner sanctum of suppliers. A tried, tested, trusted team that's been 20 years in the making.

I don't share them with just anyone! But for you – as a member – I will.

Get ready to meet:

My M&A Lawyer
The most eagle-eyed legal guy I've ever known. One session with him could spell the difference between a win and a loss.

My Due Diligence Accountant
Sellers like to hold things back, but the numbers can't lie. So it all comes out in Due Diligence – if the right accountant goes through the books.

My Finance Broker
Even today, I won't buy a business with my own money. If I need finance, I just call my broker and let him cut a deal with a specialist lender.

My Tax Advisor
We all have to pay our taxes, but no-one wants to overpay and give the taxman a bonus! So my advisor will show you how to pay your dues – and no more.

My Marketing Consultant
You'll want to fix the business you buy – starting with a marketing system that generates leads on demand. My marketing guy will show you exactly how it's done. They'll be here each time we meet. And you can hire them too!

Let them take away the guesswork, and make sure your deals go through without any hassels.

The UK has never seen a Dealmaker's Mastermind like this

Until now, options have been thin on the ground for starting out dealmakers. There are groups that operate online – but that's no way to build trust and get people to work together. There are groups for advanced dealmakers, who already know the ropes. There are groups that ignore half the market. They'll only show you how to buy a thriving business – snubbing the chance to turn around a business in distress.

There's been nothing for new dealmakers who want to learn together, work together and focus on the full range of opportunities. But now there is – and you can be part of it.

You're probably asking, why am I doing this? I'm financially independent so why go through all this effort?

Well, I'll tell you.

I've tried retiring – twice. And it's not for me. I'm a dealmaker at heart. I get a thrill from turning a business around, making it better for the staff and customers. And now, I want to start doing it on a much grander scale.

So, I'm looking for co-investors. Lots of them! And I know the best place to find them is in a Mastermind I build myself.

Throughout 2018, I will only make deals with Mastermind members. So, if you've got a deal that could use my input, bring it to me. And if it all stacks up, we can shake on it.

We'll use the Dream Team to make the deal. Plan our route to the exit. Fix the business, sell it on – and share in a fast, healthy profit.

To be clear: partnering with me is not compulsory! You'll gain the skills and confidence to make your own deals. But the option to co-invest is there, for every member.

Play by the Rules

The Mastermind has to work for everyone. So we'll all sign this Member's Charter:

1 – SHOW UP. You're expected to attend the monthly meetings in Reading and take part in our online discussions. We all contribute!

2 – SHARE. If you've had success – or failure – with a tactic or strategy, don't hold it to your chest. Others can learn from your experience.

3 – DO THE WORK. Those assignments in between meetings are not optional. Same with the actions you commit to when you're in the hotseat. You're making a commitment to the group, so we can all move on together.

4 – STAY POSITIVE. Momentum is a big part of our success. So there's no place in the room for negativity. Be realistic, of course – but we'll focus on solutions.

5 – MAKE A DEAL. Buy at least one business in the next 12 months. We can't help you turn a profit, if you won't dip a toe in the water.

The Mastermind is NOT for everyone. *Is it right for you?*

I'm looking for people with a certain mindset. So, you should only join *IF*...

- ✓ **You're decisive, and committed to building a strong financial future;**
- ✓ You have an investment mindset – ready to commit time and money;
- ✓ **You're ready to go from find to flip inside 12 months;**
- ✓ You're open to learning new ideas and letting go of bad habits;

- ✓ **You're happy to share ideas and swap opportunities; and**
- ✓ You want to strike the kind of deals where everybody wins

Do not apply if… you're the polar opposite, we're not the group for you.

We CANNOT help you *IF*…

- ✓ You're slow to make decisions, or prone to changing your mind;
- ✓ You're struggling financially;
- ✓ Your mind is closed to new ideas;
- ✓ You're looking for easy answers;
- ✓ You won't take action – you'll come back with excuses;
- ✓ You want to sit and observe, without contributing; or
- ✓ You take a hostile approach to dealmaking

If that's you, I wish you well. But I want more dynamic, more decisive people, who share our philosophy.

Financial commitment and bonuses

I'm offering three tiers of membership – choose the one that's right for you!

TIER 1: MASTERMIND

Spend the year with us, and start your dealmaking journey. You'll buy and fix at least one business, that pays you at least £10k every month until you sell it for that epic payday.

See the website for the latest prices
www.thedealmakersacademy.com

TIER 2: MASTERMIND PLUS

The full Mastermind experience, plus 5 Implementation Days

We'll make calls for you. Send emails. Set up meetings. Get you started!

If you're busy (or disorganised!) this option is for you.

See the website for the latest prices
www.thedealmakersacademy.com

TIER 3: MASTERMIND PRO (Limited Availability)

Mastermind Plus, with the ultimate extras

You'll join me at home for a day, where we'll set your financial goals and agree on a masterplan. Then, I'll attend two acquisition meetings with you. I'll act as your consultant and help you negotiate the best deal.

See the website for the latest prices
www.thedealmakersacademy.com

BONUS 1: Every member gets my entire *Dealmakers' Toolkit*

My legal team has put together a set of letters, tools and contracts to make sure you're protected. On the day you join us, you'll have access to all of this:

- ✓ Non-Disclosure Agreement;
- ✓ Asset Purchase Letter – incorporating administration offer;
- ✓ Purchase of Assets Agreement;
- ✓ Sale and Purchase Agreement;
- ✓ Detailed Offer Letter – as per a Private Equity Transaction;
- ✓ Debenture documents; and
- ✓ Due Diligence Checklist.

PLUS – the marketing templates I've developed, tested and perfected. Including:

- ✓ The Prospecting Letter I use to find sellers. You can adapt it for your niche.
- ✓ The Prospecting Letter I used to find buyers, when I flipped my last business.
- ✓ The LinkedIn Post that's brought me a ton of enquiries from sellers.

The broker I hired to sell my last business was furious when I sent out my letter – because it brought in more buyers than all his efforts combined!

BONUS 2: private online groups, for instant advice between meetings

When you're experiencing a problem, a month can feel like eternity. Fortunately, you can reach out to the group – on Facebook or WhatsApp – with any challenge, any time.

I'll be there in the groups every single day. So whatever's going on, you'll never have to wait long for an answer.

BONUS 3: free access to all my future seminars

Your seat is free at every dealmakers' seminar I run, from hereon. Stay in the loop, with all the latest deal structures, marketing updates, regulations – I'm your go-to resource, for the entirety of your dealmaking life.

Why work with me?

Remember, this is an inaugural group – the first Mastermind of its kind. And the first time I'll be sharing my dealmaking system, in intimate detail, ever!

But still, you'll want to know that I'm a safe pair of hands. So here are some comments, picked from the thousands of people I've helped in the last 20 years through coaching and training:

'After joining the mastermind group, our business has increased by over 40%. I will recommend everyone to join the mastermind group. It will add value to your business. My wife thinks I should go to Jonathan's seminar every week. She thinks Jonathan has changed my way of thinking.'

OMA EDOJA

'Had I known this stuff 20 years ago, I would be retired. I fully expect now to be increasing revenues and profits quickly across all media. Jonathan was fun, informative and open. I highly recommend training with him.'

AVRIL MILLAR

'Jonathan Jay has opened my eyes to a world of possibility. You cannot put a price on the amount of useful knowledge I have now gained and will use. One of those things you must do in a life time. Brilliant.'

RICHARD BEAN

Why Now? Why is this *URGENT*?

If you're serious about dealmaking, timing is critical. Because, I'm sure you'll want to:

- Get that first deal under your belt, and start profiting NOW;
- Get in early, while the market is still wide open – before traders and property investors jump on board;
- Be part of the only group I will *EVER* run in person; and
- Seize the (once-only) chance to work with me, as my business partner

'One of the most useful courses I have attended. I have numerous ideas that I can and will implement on Monday morning and I can't wait to see the results and growth in business this will bring! I will certainly attend another of Jonathan Jay's events in the future.'

JANE WINDLE

'The course was so fantastic that I am leaving knowing that I am in a great position. I have been enabled to apply the very best marketing techniques and I have been so inspired and motivated. I know that I can excel in the field. Thank you.'

MUNA AFSHA

'Possibly the most valuable thing I have ever attended!! And I am not just talking about training courses!! The info I have learnt on this course will make me a fortune!! 10/10.'

GARY O'NEILL

The clock is ticking… and the room is filling fast.
Are you in?

I can't push you to join – only you know whether this is right for you. But if you want a better life, financial freedom and time to enjoy your wealth, you need to make it happen somehow.

You need guidance, you need support.

And you'll get it all in the Dealmakers Mastermind.

Visualise your future

What does a 'better life' look like?

This is all about your future. So what are you striving for?

It doesn't have to be the 'high life' of fast cars, yachts and parties! If that's your thing, fine. But maybe you want something simpler?

You want to pay off your mortgage, put your children through university, build your dream home, take better holidays or support a charity.

Or maybe you want the gift of time, a chance to stop rushing, missing out on big moments and start working your own hours.

It's up to you, once you control the future.

YOUR LIFE, YOUR WAY.

'I have now gained more knowledge than I could have believed and instead of the door being closed and not knowing what to do next in my business, there is now a big shining light and my head is buzzing with ideas. Thank you, Jonathan Jay.'

KAREN McBRIDE

So… what will you be doing in the next twelve months?

Will you be back at the coalface, hoping for a better year? Or taking steps to create one, at our first ever Dealmaker's Mastermind?

Join us now. And start the most important 12 months of your life!